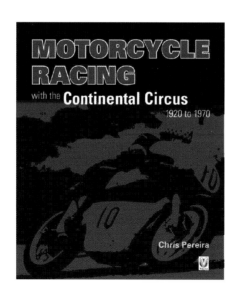

MOTORCYCLE RACING
with the **Continental Circus**
1920 to 1970

Chris Pereira

More from Veloce –

www.veloce.co.uk

First published in May 2018 by Veloce Publishing Limited, Veloce House, Parkway Farm Business Park, Middle Farm Way, Poundbury, Dorchester DT1 3AR, England. Tel +44 (0)1305 260068 / Fax 01305 250479 / e-mail info@veloce.co.uk / web www.veloce.co.uk or www.velocebooks.com. ISBN: 978-1-787112-74-2; UPC: 6-36847-01274-8.

MOTORCYCLE RACING

with the **Continental Circus**

1920 to 1970

Chris Pereira

Contents

Acknowledgements

I am once again most grateful to Rod Grainger of Veloce for publishing this book dealing with a forgotten era in motorcycle racing history. I have to thank Dan and Yvonne Shorey who devoted much time in recounting their experiences on the Continent. I must also thank Richard Morley who let me use the personal account of his 1964 Continental season. I am also grateful to Jim Curry, Raymond Ainscoe and Stefan Knittel for their assistance in obtaining photographs. For their photographic contributions I have to thank Malcolm Carling, Elwyn Roberts, Jon Day at Beaulieu, Murray's collection, Karl Schleuter, BMW AG, Karl-Heinz Reiger and Karl-Gunter Peters. I have tried to accredit all the contributors wherever possible and apologise in advance for anyone I have inadvertently left out. While I have strived to ensure historical accuracy, anomalies may inevitably appear. I would therefore welcome any authenticated corrections. Finally special thanks to my wife Sondra, for her care and support through a period of post-stroke disabilities, during the process of preparing this book for publication.

Chris Pereira

Publisher's note

We appreciate that some of the older images in this book are not of the best quality. However, we hope that the reader will appreciate that such images have been included because of their rarity and historical importance.

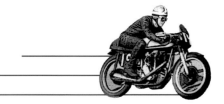

Foreword

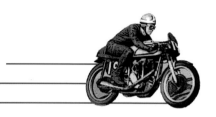

This book is dedicated to the men and women who were part of the Continental Circus during the 1950s and 1960s. Many of them had travelled halfway across the globe in the hope of finding fame and fortune. It was an extremely dangerous period in motorcycle racing history, when great courage was required to race on the many demanding and unforgiving public road circuits, which by today's standards would be totally unacceptable. As private riders they also endured hardships and conditions that would not be tolerated today. They were, however, undeterred, and determined to make the most of their newfound experiences, living nomadic lifestyles as they travelled thousands of miles between race circuits dotted across Europe. Some of them were lucky to reap the rewards by becoming World Champions or Grand Prix winners. Most of the others faded into obscurity, only to be remembered in similar books to this. Sadly, far too many lost their lives, when as many as 34 riders are known to have died while racing on the Continent during the two decades. It was this mixture of success and failure, triumph and tragedy, that was the nitty-gritty of the Continental Circus.

Chris Pereira

The term 'Continental Circus' originated with Graham Walker, prewar TT winner, Rudge works rider, and editor of *Motor Cycling* magazine. It was his description of the British riders' travels to the Continent to race in Grand Prix events in the 1920s and '30s. At the time, road racing in Britain was confined to the Isle of Man, Brooklands, Donnington, and Ireland. Consequently British riders were attracted to the Continent, where Grand Prix races took place regularly. It also provided British manufacturers with the opportunity to advertise their machines.

The excursions to the Continent began in the early 1920s, initially to France and Belgium, before spreading to Germany, Holland, Switzerland, Italy, Spain and Sweden. France is credited as being the country where motor racing began in 1906, and the first French motorcycle Grand Prix was run on the Le Mans circuit in 1920. The Belgian GP at Spa Francorchamps began in 1921, as did the German GPs at the AVUS, followed by the Sachsenring and the Nürburgring in 1927, Hockenheim in 1932 and Solitude in 1935. The Dutch TT at Assen began in 1925, and the Swiss GP at Bremgarten in 1931.

Exactly how these journeys were financed is not quite clear. Most of the riders were professionals under contract to a manufacturer, who presumably covered the basic expenses, and, on arrival in the country, the local agent provided some assistance with transport and accommodation. Some riders were contracted to use a particular brand of oil, for which they probably received a performance-related bonus. Surprisingly enough, a few of the successful prewar riders did very well financially,

Alec Bennett, the first successful British rider on the Continent. He won the French GP on a Sunbeam in 1921 and 1922. Later, riding Nortons, he won the Belgian and French in 1924, the Belgian in 1925, and the French in 1926.

often earning more than some of the early postwar riders.

While on the subject of finances, it is interesting to compare the two periods. The multi-million pound contracts paid out today have no comparison with the prewar and early postwar periods. However, some prewar riders earned quite considerable sums. For example: for his 1938 Junior TT win and 2nd place in the Senior TT, Stanley Woods is reputed to have earned in excess of £900.00 in prize money, trade bonuses and so on, which compares favourably with what factory riders earn today at the TT. Stanley Woods, however, was well known as a shrewd

Graham Walker (Rudge) winner of the 1930 500cc Dutch TT.

businessman. By contrast, Continental Circus privateers in the '50s and '60s were sometimes hard pushed to make ends meet.

With the exception of a few riders, like Eric Fernihough, who travelled to the Continent with a racing machine strapped to the running boards of their Bentleys or such like, the majority were obliged to drag themselves and their machines around the Continent by train. This rather complicated process required implicit faith in the intercontinental rail systems, to deliver machines at the appointed time and destination. It also involved having to run the gauntlet of customs officials at border crossings, the stamping of Carnets, and numerous other formalities before they eventually arrived at their destination. In his

excellent book *Continental Circus*, the late Ted Mellors describes the highs and the lows, the trials and tribulations, faced by these pioneers of racing on the Continent.

The first Continental GP season began in 1920 with the French GP run on the Le Mans circuit, followed by the Belgian GP on the well known Spa Francorchamps circuit. The British invasion began in 1921, when Alec Bennett (Sunbeam) won the 500cc class at the French GP and Hubert Hassall (Norton) the Belgian GP. Some of the other early British riders were Victor Horseman and Graham Walker (Nortons), Tommy de la Hay (Sunbeam) and Bert le Vack (Indian). Over the next few years more British riders ventured over to the Continent, and extended their activities to take in the GPs in

Germany, Italy, Switzerland and Sweden. During the early 1920s, Alec Bennett (Sunbeam) was the most successful, winning the French in 1921 and 1922, and then, on Nortons, the Belgian and French in 1924, the Belgian in 1925 and the French in 1926. Other successful British riders were Jimmy Simpson (AJS), Wal Handley on the Swiss (Motosacoche), and Stanley Woods who joined Norton in 1926.

In 1927, riding the new Walter Moore designed camshaft CS1 Norton, Stanley Woods won the Dutch, Belgian and Swiss GPs, but in 1928, due to an engine design fault, Norton results on the Continent were poor. This eventually led to Walter Moore leaving Norton for NSU, and Joe Craig taking over his job. The redesigned Norton CS1 finally won the Spanish GP at the end of the 1929 season ridden by new team member, young Percy (Tim) Hunt. The 1930 Norton team now consisted of Stanley Woods, Jimmy Simpson and Tim Hunt. Success on the Continent was brief, with a win in the Swedish GP by Simpson, who later broke a leg in the French GP at Pau after a collision with a cyclist who crossed the track during practice. The race was won by Stanley Woods on a prototype of the 1931 works bike.

The charismatic Walter Handley, who put up some superb performances on the Continent riding a Swiss Motosacoche, seen here on a Rudge in the 1930 Senior TT. (Courtesy Beaulieu Archives)

Norton domination began in 1931, after the introduction of the new classic camshaft engines designed by Arthur Carroll and Joe Craig, together with a 'Dream Team' consisting of Stanley Woods, Jimmy Guthrie, Tim Hunt and Jimmy Simpson. Such a formidable team has never been seen since. Imagine a Moto GP team consisting of Valentino Rossi, Jorge Lorenzo, Marc Marquez, and Danny Pedrosa. At first the 350 and 500cc classes were dominated by the Norton duo of

Talented Percy (Tim) Hunt who won several Continental GPs on Nortons in the 1930s, seen here in the 1931 Junior TT. (Courtesy Murray's Collection)

Stanley Woods (Norton) double winner in the 1933 Dutch TT.

Stanley Woods and Tim Hunt, who took it in turns to win each class with a total of 16 GPs between them, while Jimmy Simpson won a further 12 GPs. Unfortunately, the Woods/Hunt partnership ended in 1933 at the Swedish GP. While the pair were lapping a group of riders, Tim Hunt ran into the back of one rider who had suddenly slowed, and sustained serious injuries that ended his racing career. Stanley Woods left the team in 1933 after a disagreement over team orders, and Jimmy Simpson retired in 1934 after winning the 350 Ulster GP. Fortunately, Norton found a worthy successor in the brilliant ex-AJS Scottish rider Jimmy Guthrie, who, over the next five years, won a total of 14 GPs until his untimely death in 1937,

while leading on the last lap of the German GP at the Sachsenring. A memorial to him still stands by the original Sachsenring circuit, near to where he crashed.

During the 1930s, racing on the Continent took place most frequently in Germany, mainly due to considerable investment in development and technology by the three main manufacturers: BMW, DKW, and NSU. Apart from the main GP circuits, Germany had numerous others, including the Dreieckrennen, where three public roads were joined together to form a temporary circuit, and on which National Championship series were run. These national races were dominated by the supercharged BMWs of Karl Gall and Otto Ley, the 250cc supercharged two-stroke DKWs of Arthur Geiss and Walfred Winkler, the 500cc DKWs of Kurt Mansfield and Karl Bodmer, and the NSUs of Heiner Fleischmann and Wilhelm Herz. BMW GP superiority began in 1936, when Karl Gall and Otto Ley won the 1936 Dutch and Swedish, and the 1937 Dutch and German GPs. In 1938, George Meier, who had replaced Otto Ley, won the Belgian, Dutch, German, and Italian GPs.

Germany was not admitted into the FIM (Fédération Internationale de Motocyclisme) until after the war, and so races in Germany were not open to FIM riders. Nevertheless,

The invincible Jimmy Guthrie (Norton) who won a total of 14 GPs between 1934 and 1937, seen here in typical forceful style in the 1934 Senior TT. (Courtesy Murray's Collection)

Jimmy Simpson (Norton) winning the 1934 350cc Dutch TT.

Walter Rusk leading Jimmy Guthrie on Nortons in the 1936 Swiss GP.

Jimmy Guthrie (Norton) at the 1937 Dutch TT, with Joe Craig, Freddie Frith, and Crasher White.

Otto Ley leading Karl Gall in the 1936 Swedish GP.
(Courtesy BMW AG)

BMW works rider Wiggerl Kraus in 1938.
(Courtesy BMW AG)

The start line at Schleiz in 1937 with the BMWs of #59 Karl Gall and #60 Otto Ley flanked by the DKWs of Karl Bodmer and Kurt Mansfield. (Courtesy BMW AG)

George Meier (BMW) winning the 1938 Belgian GP. (Courtesy BMW AG)

racing continued in Germany. The 500cc class in these national events were dominated by the supercharged BMWs of George Meier and Ludwig Kraus. They were challenged by the supercharged four-cylinder NSU of Heiner Fleischmann, who was involved in several epic duels with Meier's BMW. The 250/350cc classes were still dominated by the supercharged two-stroke DKWs of Hermann Paul Müller, Kurt Mansfield, Ewald Kluge and Siggi Wünsche and the 350cc supercharged twin cylinder NSU of Wilhelm Hertz. The main contender in the sidecar class, was Herman Bohm with the four-cylinder NSU. This situation continued until 1951 when Germany was re-admitted to the FIM, and many of the German circuits became available for International events. BMW superiority unfortunately ended due to the postwar FIM ban on superchargers. The first major postwar International event in Germany was the non-championship German Grand Prix in August 1951, on the Solitude circuit just

Wilhelm Herz on a 350cc supercharged NSU at Hockenheim in 1948. (Courtesy Karl-Heinz Reiger)

outside Stuttgart, where Geoff Duke scored a double 350/500 win on works Nortons. Earlier Ken Kavanagh had won the 350 race at the Schottenring and Eric Oliver the sidecar race at Hockenheim.

The Continental Circus came to an end with the onset of WW2, but was revived in the early 1950s. At this time it was mainly private riders from Britain and the former Commonwealth countries of Australia, New Zealand, South Africa and Canada, who formed the bulk of the Continental Circus participants.

The life of the Continental Circus rider in the '50s and '60s was potentially dangerous right from the start, with the ever-present threat of serious injury or death. Most of the circuits they raced on were, by today's standards, lethal public road circuits, surrounded by street furniture, houses, brick walls, and often with indifferent surfaces, ranging from cobblestones to traffic-polished roads, which were extremely slippery when wet. Not for them today's purpose-built Moto GP circuits, with their run-off areas, gravel traps and excellent medical facilities. A total of 34 riders and passengers, including world champions and title contenders, are known to

Sri Lankan rider Rally Dean (350 Norton) at Silverstone.

have lost their lives on the Continent during these two decades.

Circus riders led essentially nomadic lives as they travelled round Europe from circuit to circuit. A serious injury or a major engine blow-up could significantly reduce their earning capacity. Riders also had to maintain their own machines, as well as their transporters, and major engine rebuilds in a paddock were not unusual. Fortunately, many of the German meetings were attended by a mobile workshop with excellent engineering facilities that were available to riders. The riders also had to rely on the goodwill of the race shops back in England to dispatch spare parts to them in response to an urgent telephone call.

Wives and girlfriends also played a very important supporting role – they usually looked after the paperwork, entries and such like, and often shared the driving on the long journeys between race meetings. There are several examples in the history of the Continental Circus of husband and wife or girlfriend racing partnerships. Starting with the early postwar period there were the British partnerships of Eric and Joan Briggs, Tommy and Ginger Wood, Phil Heath and his wife. They were followed later by Dickie and Phyllis Dale, Frank and Rita Perris, Lewis Young and Carol Steed, Dan and Yvonne Shorey and several others.

The Commonwealth riders usually had wives or girlfriends to keep them company during the long months away from home. Some of the more well known were Ray and Jill Amm, Maurie and Betty Quincey, Paddy and Janet Driver, Tom

The Swiss rider Rudi Kurth with English passenger Dane Rowe.

and Betty Phillis, Jim and Marlene Redman, the previous two also having young children with them, Jack Findlay and Nanou Layonnard, Jack and Betty Ahearn and several others. In 1955, Bob Brown was probably the envy of the paddock when he had two young Australian ladies travelling with him.

There were also the sidecar racing partnerships of John and Kathy Tickle, Australians Ray and Jean Foster, Jacques Drion and Inge Stoll, and Rudi Kurth and Dane Rowe. Marie Lambert competed as passenger with her husband, the Swiss driver Claude Lambert, but she was sadly killed in an accident at the 1961 TT. Within these Circus communities, the juxtaposition of fairly basic living accommodation in the crowded paddocks inevitably created friendships and a sense of camaraderie, in which riders often helped each other and socialised together at post-race celebrations.

It was not long before British riders were joined by riders from Australia and New Zealand, who would come over to ride in the TT, and spend the rest of the year racing on the Continent.

Some of the early 'colonial types' as they were sometimes referred to, were the Australians Harry Hinton, George Morrison, Eric McPherson and New Zealander Sid Jensen in 1949. Over the next few years, they were followed by a steady influx of Antipodean riders including Rod Coleman, Ken Kavanagh, Tony McAlpine, Ken Mudford, Ernie Ring, Gordon Laing and Keith Campbell. From South Africa, Ray Amm and Rudi Allison.

Among them was lone Sri Lankan rider Rally Dean, who spent a couple of years racing a pair of Nortons on the Continent. He was married to a former Isle of Man beauty queen, and lived in Birmingham during the winter, working in the Norton race shop. His Nortons often benefitted from special works bits, which made them slightly faster than average. As Phil Heath recalled "I borrowed Rally Dean's 500 Norton for the Belgian Grand Prix, and was surprised at how much quicker it was than my own."

Birmingham-born Harry Hinton's reputation as Australia's most successful rider engineer had preceded him. In spite of having lost one eye at the age of 20, he had dominated racing in Australia both prewar and postwar. He also had an enviable reputation for extracting phenomenal performance from his race engines. George Morrison was a motorcycle dealer, and also a gifted mechanic, who joined forces with Harry Hinton for their trips to the Continent.

The first postwar Australian rider was Eric McPherson on a 358cc AJS, seen here at Kate's Cottage in the 1950 Senior TT.

Eric McPherson was a motorcycle salesman from Sydney, who had started racing prewar. On his first visit to the TT in 1948, riding a 7R AJS, he crashed during practice on the exit from Governor's Bridge after hitting a patch of oil, and sustained injuries which kept him out of the races.

The three Australians upheld their reputations with good results on the Continent. At Gedinne in July 1949, Hinton and Morrison had staged a dead heat finish to win the 500cc race. All three riders were rewarded with works rides, Hinton and Morrison with Norton, and McPherson with AJS, whose 5th places in the Dutch TT and Belgian GP, plus 4th place in the Ulster, gave him

almost equal 4th place in the 1949 350cc World Championships.

Following home success, Sid Jensen was selected as New Zealand's representative to the TT, which he justified with 5th place in the Senior TT on a GP Triumph.

One of the British pioneers of the postwar Continental Circus was Fergus Anderson who had also raced on the Continent before the war. From as early as 1947 he did most of his racing on the Continent, riding a 500 Norton and a MkVIII KTT Velocette, which was replaced by a 7R AJS in 1948, and a 250 Guzzi. He eventually went to live in Italy, and established a good relationship with Moto Guzzi that was to last for several years, and ensured a steady supply of works machines. An outspoken and often controversial figure, Fergus Anderson wrote an insightful series of articles in *The Motor Cycle* in the 1950s, called 'Continental Circus,' in which many interesting background details were revealed.

Some of the other early postwar private British riders on the Continent were Ernie Thomas, David Whitworth, Jock Weddel, Eric Oliver, Tommy Wood,

Albert Moule, Phil Heath and Eric Briggs. In the meantime, both Norton and Velocette continued to send their respective works riders, Harold Daniel and Artie Bell, Ken Bills, Bob Foster and Freddie Frith to the Dutch, Belgian and Swiss GPs, although these events had yet to achieve World Championship status.

It must be remembered that during these two decades, participation in the World Championships by private riders was sustainable. There was still a perceptible career path towards a World Championship for the more determined and successful. Riders from many different walks of life set off on the World Championship trail, many of them with ambitions towards fame and glory and the ultimate goal of a world title. History has shown that this was still within the bounds of possibility during that time, the names of Keith Campbell, Tom Phillis and Jim Redman springing to mind. All these riders, including the slightly less ambitious, decided to earn their living racing motorcycles. This involved travelling round the Continent, from Finland in the north to Spain in the south, Holland in the west to

New Zealander Rod Coleman who later rode for AJS, seen at May Hill Ramsey in the Senior TT, 1953.

Czechoslovakia and Yugoslavia in the east, moving from circuit to circuit, country to country, circus fashion, earning their living from racing; ergo Continental Circus.

Riding in World Championship events, however, had certain advantages and good results could lead to an invitation to join a factory team. However, most of the privateers earned their bread and butter from the many non-championship national events, which took place all over the Continent. Provided they did reasonably well during the season, most of the Antipodean riders could usually pay for their passage back home, taking their machines with them. The bikes were sold to local riders, and helped to pay for new machines for the following season which were purchased from the factories in advance, and then collected on arrival in England.

The obvious choices of machine for private riders during the early postwar period were the 350 and 500cc single overhead camshaft Manx Nortons that became available in 1947. The plunger framed, or 'garden gate' models as they were known, had the latest hydraulic damped Roadholder forks, but were prone to frame breakages. The engines were updated in 1949 to double overhead camshaft operation. The prewar MkVIII KTT Velocette was produced in limited numbers, and not as readily available, but was the preferred choice among 350cc riders, until its production ended in 1949.

In 1948, AMC introduced the 350cc 7R AJS, or

The 1951 Velocette team at Floreffe: Cecil Sandford, Bill Lomas, and Bob Foster.

'Boy Racer' as it was known, which went through several changes over the years. Another 500cc machine was the twin cylinder GP Triumph that went on sale in 1948. It was based on Ernie Lyon's special 1946 Senior MGP winning machine, prepared by Fred Clark. Production versions had light alloy head and barrels, as used on the wartime generators. These four machines became the essential tools of the Circus rider, both in Britain and among Continental riders.

The superiority of the 500 Manx Norton was established as early as 1947, when Fergus Anderson had wins at Floreffe, Mettet and Albi. The KTT Velocette proved very successful in the hands of Tommy Wood, David Whitworth and Reg Armstrong. In 1948 David Whitworth won the 350 race at Brusselles, and Eric Oliver won the 350 race at Floreffe. Tommy Wood had wins in 1949 at Pau, the Spanish GP, Erlen and Olten. Despite reports of wayward steering and the idiosyncratic rear sprung hub, the GP Triumph was reasonably successful, ridden by David Whitworth, Reg Armstrong, and Belgian Auguste Goffin. According to Syd Barnett, who raced a GP Triumph on British short circuits with some success during the early '50s, "The GP Triumph was quite fast in its day, although the steering tended to get a bit lively, I fitted a fork brace to mine, which cured the problem." The best results for the GP Triumph were New Zealander Sid Jensen's 5th place in the 1949 Senior TT, and Don Crossley's win in the 1948 Senior Manx. The 7R AJS was slow to gain popularity until the KTT Velo went out of production, but achieved some success with veteran rider Bill Petch, and the Belgian riders Goffin and Erge.

Apart from the World Championship GPs, the sidecar classes in the Continental Circus during the early 1950s did not attract many British privateers, with the exception of Eric Oliver and Cyril Smith with their Norton outfits. Between 1948 and the early 1950s, Eric Oliver with passengers Denis Jenkinson, and later Lorenzo Dobelli, dominated the Circus with wins at Floreffe, Mettet, Chimay, Geddine, and others. He was joined in 1952 by Cyril Smith and passenger Bob Clements, who went on to win the World Championship that year. Continental opposition came mostly from Swiss Hans Haldemann, Belgian Franz Vanderschrick, and Frenchman Jacques Drion, all on Norton outfits, as well as the Italians Ercole Frigerio, Albino Milani and Ernesto Merlo, usually with Gilera Saturno outfits, and occasionally using a four-cylinder Gilera. The talented Frigerio was the main opponent to Eric Oliver, and finished 2nd to him in the 1951 World Championship, with a win in the Swiss GP, and several 2nd places. He was highly regarded by his great rival Eric Oliver, with whom he enjoyed a friendly rivalry.

Eric Oliver and Lorenzo Dobelli (Norton) at Mettet in 1951.

For private riders who depended on start money to earn a living, their earning capacity relied to a great extent on their reputation. Until they had established themselves, some riders had a hard time, and even had to exist on 'iron rations' for several weeks. The trade representatives played an important part, and could pay a fairly successful rider as much as a £200.00 retaining fee for using a particular brand of oil, with free supplies of fuel and oil at trade-supported international meetings. Other accessory manufacturers also provided support with the free supply of tyres, brake linings and such like consumables. Payment for signs on the side of vans advertising various products such as fuel, oils, tyres, chains, etc, also helped to subsidise their incomes. It must be remembered that these were the days when sponsorship from outside the industry was non-existent. Many riders had headed notepaper listing their successes when they wrote to organisers requesting a start. There was a considerable variation in 'start money' payments between organisers and countries. Most German organisers paid out generous start money and prize money, and also rewarded riders with gifts of cameras, watches, radios and such like. This was in marked contrast to some of the main GP organisers, who were particularly miserly in their payouts, even to world championship

Start of the 1950 350 Dutch TT: #50 Johnny Lockett (Norton), #52 Geoff Duke (Norton), #51 Dickie Dale (Norton), #79 Bill Lomas (Velocette), and #60 Les Graham (AJS).

Dickie Dale (Norton) leading Johnny Lockett (Norton) at the 350 Dutch TT in 1950.

contenders, on the grounds that they were obliged to ride anyway to earn world championship points. Being the poor relations, and often less well paid, sidecar drivers did not qualify for special grants, and were particularly hard-pressed, having to provide for their passengers as well.

In the days when border controls still existed, border crossings often proved difficult, requiring a great deal of tact and patience to navigate. Some riders went out of their way to choose less well-known crossings. Firstly, a Carnet de Passage was required for each machine, and this had to be stamped in and out of each country. Entry visas were required by some countries, and sometimes these were only provided on proof by the organisers of race entries. In the days before mobile phones, emails etc, communication with race organisers for confirmation of entries and start money must have been extremely difficult. When all of these administrative problems had been overcome, with a great sense of relief, the actual riding was probably the easy bit.

Continental circuits varied considerably in nature. There were the main enclosed Grand Prix circuits such as Assen, Spa Francorchamps, Hockenheim, the Nürburgring, and Bremgarten, for instance, which mainly hosted the GPs. There were also international events on public road circuits such as Floreffe, Mettet, Gedinne

in Belgium, Luxembourg, St Wendel, Salzburg in Austria, Hedemora in Sweden, and so on. These international events were usually administered by the respective National Federations. There were also the minor temporary circuits in or just outside small villages, that were probably promoted by the local town council or motorcycle club. These circuits sprang up overnight, with local roads being closed off, and rope barriers and straw bales installed to form a circuit. Despite their rudimentary nature, these meetings were very hospitable towards foreign riders, who were often feted and offered free accommodation in the local hotel or in private homes. Likewise, paddock conditions varied considerably from circuit to circuit, ranging from paved paddocks with showers and toilets, to a grassy field that may or may not have had a standpipe for water, and not much else.

From the early 1950s, the international meetings at Floreffe and Mettet, usually run in April each year, became popular as pre-season testing grounds for many of the British and continental factory teams. In 1950, Les Graham (works AJS) won the 350 race at Mettet. Bill Doran (works AJS) won the 350 race at Floreffe, and Les Graham won the 500 race. In 1951, Cecil Sandford (works Velocette) won the 350 race at Floreffe and Reg Armstrong (works AJS) the 500 race. At Mettet

Programme cover from Mettet, May 1st, 1955.

Bill Doran (works AJS) won the 350 race and Geoff Duke (works Norton) the 500 race. In 1952 Rod Coleman (works AJSs) had a double win at Mettet.

With Germany having been re-admitted into the FIM, NSU began to send its works riders to these circuits, as well as Moto Guzzi, which was usually represented by Fergus Anderson and Enrico Lorenzetti. At Floreffe in 1953, Bill Lomas (works NSU) won the 250 race, Syd Lawton (works Norton) the 350 and Ken Kavanagh (works Norton) the 500, while at Mettet, Derek Farrant (works AJS) won the 350 and Les Graham now on MV, won the 500 race. In the sidecar class, Eric Oliver (Norton) usually won most years at both circuits.

The Floreffe circuit situated southwest of Namur was 8.45 miles (13.6km) long. It had several long straights, with fast corners running through pine forest, and passing through small villages until a tricky twisty section through the village of Buzzet. The lap record set in 1950 by Les Graham on the Porcupine AJS was 88mph (141.59km/h). It was considered to be quite a dangerous circuit, and following Fergus Anderson's fatal accident in 1956, the Belgian federation banned any further racing at this circuit. A large memorial to Fergus Anderson remains in the town of Buzzet.

The Mettet circuit was 5.2 miles (8.4km) long and consisted basically of two triangles joined together. The unique feature of the circuit was the crossroads where the two triangles joined. The two roads were separated by a wire fence with the riders racing on either side in opposite directions. It was a circuit that favoured fast machines with 500cc lap speeds in the early '50s, of 95mph (152km/h).

Apart from Floreffe and Mettet, Continental Circus riders had a vast selection of circuits to choose from. Pau and Albi in France, Chimay, Gedinne and Limbourg in Belgium, Erlen, Olten, Berne and Lausanne in Switzerland, Zandvoort and Tubbergen in Holland, and in Scandinavia Hedemora, Turku, and Helsinki, amongst many others. In 1951, with Germany's inclusion, many new circuits were added to the calendar, mainly the Nuburgring, Hockenheim, Solitude, and the Schottenring.

The early postwar availability of cheap ex-War Department (WD) vehicles encouraged many 'privateers,' as they became known, to abandon the complexities of rail travel in favour of road transport. Ex-Army three-ton trucks, ambulances and Luton body vans were pressed into service, and some of them were even converted to provide living and sleeping accommodation. Most of these vehicles had a very low cruising speed, around 40mph, and together with the state of the roads on the Continent in the pre-motorway days, travelling between circuits as far apart as Finland and Spain involved long hours on the road. Many of these ex-WD vehicles were still in use well into the mid 1950s. In 1955, I travelled to the Silverstone 'Saturday' meeting in the back of South African rider Eddie Grant's converted ex-RAF ambulance. As late as 1957 ex-world champion Cecil Sandford was using a Commer J type 15cwt for his journeys to the Continent. From personal experience, as an employee of A R Taylor Garages, I was sometimes called upon to transport Cecil Sandford's machines to race meetings. I recall taking the works Mondials to Silverstone for the 1957 Hutchinson 100, and I was left in no doubt that this type of van was a vast improvement on Eddie Grant's ambulance and such like.

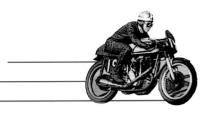

In 1951 the new Featherbed Nortons went on sale to the public, and the prospect of enjoying superior road-holding made them very popular with riders. Despite the hype, the quality of the production Manx Norton was rather patchy. While some riders were lucky to get a good model, many ended up with one that left something to be desired. There were reports of conrod failures, frequent valve spring breakages, and unsatisfactory rear damper units. Irish rider Manliffe Barrington crashed while flat out at the Cronk-y-voddy crossroads during TT practice in 1952, allegedly due to a conrod failure, and received injuries that ended his racing career. Phil Heath suffered a similar fate at the Dutch TT, and ended up in a ditch with multiple injuries, again due to a conrod failure on his Norton. In spite of these problems, the 350 and 500cc Featherbed Nortons were the only machines available to private riders that were capable of achieving good results during the 1950s.

Ray Amm was probably the most successful privateer during the early 1950s, with a 350/500 double win at Luxembourg in May 1952, plus 350cc wins at the Schotten and the Grenzland Ring. Belgian Auguste Goffin had switched to Norton, scoring double wins at Montauban and Geddine. Big Australian Tony McAlpine had a 350/500 double win at Van Elten in Holland, and New Zealander Dene Hollier had a double win at Tubbergen. AJS 7R rider Bill Petch had wins at Marseilles, Hockenheim and the AVUS. Some of the successful private Norton riders during 1953 were Ray Amm, John Storr, Gordon Laing,

Frenchman Jacques Collot, and German Rudi Knees.

Among them was future World Champion, Australian Keith Campbell, in his first year on the Continent riding his KTT Velocette and 500cc Norton. He was well known for having rather scruffy looking machines, which often seemed to be in need of mechanical attention. On the Velocette he had wins at Vesoul and Seraing, and also won the 500cc races at Vesoul, Tubbergen and Agen. Suspended until mid-1956 for his part in the Dutch TT strike, Keith obtained a downgraded licence that allowed him to ride in non-international events, which kept his finances afloat. He was particularly successful in Scandinavia, which included winning the 350 Finnish GP at Helsinki in 1955, the 1956 350cc Swedish GP, and was 2nd to Geoff Duke's Gilera in the 500cc race. He also had 500cc wins at St Wendel and Chimay in 1956, before recording his first win for Moto Guzzi at Senigallia in July.

Eric Oliver continued to dominate the Circus sidecar events during 1952, with wins at Pau, Mettet, Norisring, Hamburg, Avignon, and the non-championship French GP at Albi, in spite of an early season crash at Bordeaux, when he and Dobelli each broke a leg. At the Belgian GP, his leg was still in plaster, and Dobelli was still on crutches, but with a volunteer passenger, he fought a race-long battle with Albino Milani's four-cylinder Gilera, forcing his way past at the La Source hairpin on the last lap, and beating him to the line. Unfortunately, in spite of his valiant efforts, due to a series of mechanical problems, he could finish no higher than 4th in the World Championship. Eric Oliver's main rival from 1951, the talented Gilera driver, Ercole Frigerio, was unfortunately killed in the Swiss GP at Bremgarten, when he went off the road and hit a tree. The Bremgarten circuit, as the name suggests, was set in a wooded area with many trees bordering the circuit, and had claimed the lives of several riders, including Omobono Tenni and Dave Bennett. The other British Norton sidecar exponent, Cyril Smith, first with passenger Bob Clements, had wins at Luxembourg, Chimay and the AVUS. Following his excellent win in the German GP at Solitude he was loaned a works Norton engine, and then, with Les Nutt as passenger, he went on to win the Sidecar World Championship. The two British drivers were usually followed by Swiss Hans Haldemann and Frenchman Jacques Drion, also using Norton outfits. Drion had moved to Aachen in 1952, and teamed up with Inge Stoll, who became the first International female sidecar passenger. Inge was married to Manfred Grunwald, the passenger to BMW driver Fritz Hillebrand.

For 1953 Eric Oliver had two outfits, one of which was the revolutionary fully streamlined outfit with integral sidecar and kneeling riding position, which later led to the almost universal adoption of the 'kneeler' riding position. The streamlined outfit was only used in the Belgian GP, when it was discovered that it was unstable on the long fast Masta section, and required constant steering correction to keep it in a straight line. The two Norton stalwarts, Eric Oliver with new passenger Stan Dibben, and Cyril Smith with Les Nutt, were now starting to come under pressure from the German BMW drivers, Willi Noll, Wiggerl Kraus and Fritz Hillebrand. However, the two Norton drivers continued to dominate most of the Circus events. It was not unusual to see the two Nortons leading a pack of BMWs. A familiar sight was Eric Oliver in a full opposite lock drift on a left-hand corner, leading one of the BMWs with their understeering right-hand sidecar outfit. According to Stan Dibben, who rode with Eric Oliver as well as Cyril Smith, Eric's advantage on left-hand corners was due to his long arms and lanky build, that gave him the extra leverage for steering and also enabled him

Eric Oliver and Lorenzo Dobelli with their oversteering (Norton), ahead of the understeering BMW of Wiggerl Kraus at Hockenheim in 1951.

to move his body further into the sidecar on left-hand corners. The 1953 World Championship was eventually decided in the final round at Monza, where Eric Oliver and Stan Dibben won by half a

wheel from Cyril Smith and Bob Clements, while Jacques Drion and Inge Stoll finished third on Eric Oliver's streamlined outfit.

1957 World Champion Fritz Hillebrand and Manfred Grunwald (BMW) in the German GP at Hockenheim.
(Courtesy Karl-Heinz Reiger)

Under the direction of Edgar Franks, the production Manx Nortons underwent major changes in 1954 to short-stroke dimensions: the 350 to 76x76.7mm, and the 500 to 86x85.6mm bore and stroke, plus many other changes. One of the biggest problems suffered by the new models was persistent upper bevel gear drive failure. In the words of South African rider Eddie Grant, in his first year in Europe with one of the new 500 Nortons, "I had to carry spare sets of bevel gears and change them after every couple of meetings." In fact the general opinion of many private riders was that when one bought a new Manx Norton, before you raced it you had to, amongst other things, change the bevel gears, modify the timing side main bearing, and change the standard rear suspension units for a proprietary brand. Conrod failures had not been entirely eliminated,

Otto Daiker (NSU) leading Siggi Wunsche (DKW) at Solitude in 1953. (Courtesy Karl-Heinz Reiger)

*Maurie Quincey (Norton) leading
Auguste Goffin (Norton) at
St Wendel 1954.
(Courtesy Karl-Heinz Reiger)*

*Privateer battle in the 1954 Belgian GP. Jack Ahearn, Auguste Goffin and Maurie Quincey on Nortons, leading Peter
Murphy's (AJS). (Courtesy Maurie Quincey)*

Start at Feldberg 1954: #23 Maurie Quincey (Norton), #21 Walter Zeller (BMW), and #22 Tommy Wood (Norton).
(Courtesy Maurie Quincey)

as Eric Hinton discovered when his 350 Norton broke its conrod near Ballaugh during the 1956 Junior TT, casting him off and causing injuries that put him out of the Senior TT. Riding a semi-works Norton in the 1955 Senior TT, Maurie Quincey crashed on the approach to the 33rd milestone due to a broken connecting rod, and suffered serious injuries that put an end to his European ambitions. In response to some of these problems, during 1956 and 1957 Nortons finally changed to coarse pitch bevels to cure the bevel gear failures, and also modified the timing side main bearing.

In the 1951 Senior Manx GP, Robin Sherry had finished 4th on a Matchless that was based on the roadster twin-cylinder engine, mounted in a AJS 7R frame – the brainchild of Ike Hatch of AMC. The following year, Australian Ernie Ring rode a similar prototype Matchless in the Senior TT, but fell off on the last lap. Derek Farrant won the 1952 Senior Manx GP on the same machine, which formed the basis of the Matchless G45 racer that went into production in 1953. At first the G45 appeared to offer a slightly less expensive alternative to the Manx Norton, and achieved a modicum of success on British short circuits, ridden by Michael O'Rourke, John Clark, Derek Ennett, Bob Anderson, Derek Powell, Frank Perris, and New Zealander Peter Murphy. As far as the Continental Circus was concerned, Bob Brown and Peter Murphy were probably the most successful G45 exponents. In 1954 Peter Murphy was 6th in the Belgian GP and Bob Brown was 5th in the 1955 Dutch TT. In 1957 Peter Murphy had a win at Pau, was 2nd in the non championship Swedish GP, and was also 8th in the Senior TT. The best result for a G45 was Manxman Derek Ennett's 6th place in the 1956 Senior TT at 92.66mph (149.08km/h), and the Manufacturer's team prize for AMC with team mates New Zealander Gavin Dunlop 8th and Frank Perris 14th.

The G45 itself was like the 'Curate's Egg' – good in parts, but suffered from various problems. They were difficult to start, had a narrow power band, and a characteristic stutter on full song,

Ray Amm in his fatal debut ride on a 350 MV at Imola in 1955.

probably caused by vibration affecting the carburetion. Mike O'Rourke, who raced a G45 in the TT and on short circuits during 1953, recalled: "I took delivery of one of the new G45s from the factory in 1953, and took it straight over to the Island for the TT. In its shake-down race it went reasonably well, but I retired due to a broken fuel pipe. I then went to the Dutch TT, and, in keeping with the times, I rode the G45 down to Assen, and my uncle Jim Oliver rode my 7R, while my wife and aunt followed in an A40 shooting brake with the tools and equipment. Unfortunately, I fell off in the 350 race and did not ride the G45. I then rode it on short circuit during the rest of 1953. It did not handle as well as a Norton or 7R, used to vibrate quite a bit and suffered from severe 'megaphonitis.' The early versions like mine also suffered from rapid cam wear and fracture of the rocker support pillars. On short circuits when it was going well it was as quick as a 500 Norton, and I won the Coronation Cup at Brands Hatch." Ironically, Bob McIntyre who rode G45s as part of the AMC works team in 1953, preferred it to the E95 version of the Porcupine AJS.

Until the mid-1950s, the 250cc class had been dominated by Italian and German works machines, due to the lack of new machines being produced for private sale. In 1955, NSU produced a limited number of the 250cc single cylinder Sportmax that were made available ostensibly only to riders who had won national titles. In its production form, the single overhead cam Sportmax was supplied with a beautifully sculptured hand-beaten alloy tank, and a polished aluminium fully enclosed dustbin type fairing, with a maximum speed of over 120mph. Several privateers found they now had a suitable machine with which to compete in the 250cc races on the Continent. The most successful were the former NSU works riders Hans Baltisberger and Herman-Paul Muller. Other NSU riders were Eric Hinton and Bob Brown, who rode Reg Armstrong's machine. At Brno in 1956 there was a battle for the lead between the four NSUs of Hans Baltisberger, Eric Hinton, Bob Brown and Horst Kassner, until the rain came down. First to fall off on the lethal surface was Bob Brown, followed by Eric Hinton and Baltisberger. Unfortunately, poor Baltisberger, who was also a talented Concert Pianist, succumbed to his injuries. The Sportmax proved good enough for 'Happy' Muller to win the 1955 250cc World Championship. It was also very successful in the 250cc class in Britain, ridden by John Surtees, Mike Hailwood, Sammy Miller, Tommy Robb, Dan Shorey, Jack Murgatroyd and several others, until the arrival in the 1960s of the Bultaco and Aermacchi.

The mid-1950s was the Golden Age of domination by Gilera, MV, Moto Guzzi, NSU and Mondial. During this period many British works riders, somewhat disillusioned by the lack of

Promising South African Eddie Grant on his 500 Norton at Monza in 1955. (Courtesy Karl-Heinz Reiger)

Start of the 500 race at the popular Dutch circuit of Tubbergen in 1956: #95 Eddie Grant (Norton), #78 Piet Bakker (Norton), and #1 Ernst Riedelbauch (BMW) on the front row. (Courtesy Karl-Heinz Reiger)

initiative by the British manufacturers, joined the Italian teams, for which some of them received some totally unjustified criticism. Norton teamster Reg Armstrong joined Gilera in 1953, and was soon followed by Geoff Duke, who had not been able to agree favourable terms with Norton Director Gilbert Smith. Norton's loss was Gilera's gain. This exodus to Continental teams provided opportunities for some of the privateers, such as Rhodesian Ray Amm, South African Rudi Allison, Australians Gordon Laing, Maurie Quincey, Ernie Ring, and New Zealander Ken Mudford, to get works rides with Norton and AJS. Ken Kavanagh moved from Norton to Moto Guzzi in 1954, and Ray Amm, tired of continuously riding on the limit and beyond to keep up with the Italian opposition, left Norton and joined MV in 1955, but was sadly killed during his debut ride at Imola on a 350 MV.

Unfortunately there were several fatal accidents during the early 1950s. The talented and very promising Birmingham rider Dave Bennett was recruited into the Norton works team for 1952, following his win in the Senior Manx GP and some impressive performances at National meetings in 1951. In his Grand Prix debut at the Swiss GP on the Bremgarten circuit, he was involved in a battle for the lead with AJS riders Bill Doran and Jack Brett, when he went off the road, hit a tree and succumbed to his injuries. This prompted the suggestion that some young riders were being brought into works teams too early, putting them under too much pressure to produce good results.

Riding a works AJS Porcupine, Australian Ernie Ring was killed during the 1953 Belgian GP when he crashed near Malmedy. The following year, promising Australian Gordon Laing was also killed in the Belgian GP riding a works Norton. Well known British privateer Denis Lashmar, often associated with the Pike BSAs, was killed in the 1954 German GP at Solitude. Having already won the 125cc World Championship, NSU works rider Rupert Hollaus, was killed during practice for the Italian GP at Monza in 1954 when he crashed at the Lesmo curve.

The need for the privateers to negotiate reasonable start money terms with organisers was a constant battle. This rather contentious issue finally came to a head at the Dutch TT in 1955. It is alleged that the private riders were unable to agree start money terms in advance as usual. Having duly arrived at the circuit and on race day, they were offered derisory amounts, considerably less than they would have received at other minor events. The Dutch TT was run on an enclosed circuit, and the KNMV stood to recoup large profits from estimated attendance figures of 100,000. Although the riders had expressed their dissatisfaction, the organisers, the KNMV, chose to ignore it. The private riders then threatened to pull in after one lap of the 350 race, but the organisers regarded it as an idle threat. The private riders called their bluff, and pulled in after one lap, threatening to do the same in the 500 race unless the organisers increased their offer. A small increased offer was then made to cover both races, which was rejected by the riders, who then obtained the support of Geoff Duke and the Gilera team. Faced with the possibility of another debacle, the organisers backed down. More favourable terms were agreed and the 500 race went ahead as planned. The reason for the support of Geoff Duke and the Gilera team goes back to an incident at the Italian Grand Prix in 1953, when the organisers refused to pay starting money to the British riders of Italian works teams. Fergus Anderson, ever a controversial figure, organised a petition condemning this action. It was signed by all the works riders, and supported by the privateers as well. The organisers backed down and the riders were paid.

Following the Dutch incident, the KNMV vented their fury by referring the matter to the CSI (Commission Sportive Internationale) of the sport's governing body the FIM. The autocratic FIM was made up of powerful National federations, circuit owners and such like, who were seldom sympathetic to the needs of the riders. Consequently, summary suspensions were handed out, ranging from four to six months, to Geoff Duke, Reg Armstrong, Giuseppe Colnago, Alfredo Milani and Umberto Masetti. Also private riders, Australians Jack Ahearn, Keith Campbell, Bob Brown, and Tony McAlpine, and New Zealanders Peter Murphy, John Hempleman and Barry

Stormont. The consequences of these suspensions were to affect the future of all these riders in one way or another.

In 1956, Moto Guzzi had to find a replacement for Ken Kavanagh. Their first recruit was South African rider Eddie Grant, who had been putting up some good performances on his private Nortons. He was given a works Guzzi for the 350 German GP at Solitude, where he was amongst the front runners until he fell off without injury. He next rode a works Guzzi at Senigallia, where he finished 5th in the 350cc race, which was won by another new Guzzi recruit Keith Campbell. He was no doubt in line to join the Moto Guzzi team, but unfortunately crashed his 350 Norton at Villefranche-de-Rouergue on 5th August, and though not seriously injured, he died of exposure due to lack of medical attention. The next Moto Guzzi recruit was talented 26-year-old, Manxman Derek Ennett, who was sadly killed in the 1956 350cc Ulster GP, during his debut ride. Moto Guzzi finally succeeded when they recruited successful Australian Continental Circus riders Keith Campbell and Keith Bryan in 1957. Keith Campbell justified his selection by winning the 1957 350cc World Championship, while Keith Bryan achieved podium places in the Belgian and Ulster GPs.

Unlucky Eddie Grant on a works 350 Guzzi in the 1956 German GP.

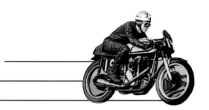

Following the withdrawal of Gilera, Moto Guzzi and Mondial from Grand Prix racing at the end of 1957, the major Grand Prix contenders faced a completely different situation at the beginning of 1958. Some ex-works riders decided to retire, but fortunately for the future of Grand Prix racing, ex-world champions, Geoff Duke, Keith Campbell and his Guzzi team-mate Dickie Dale, decided to go back to being private riders. These riders now had their reputations at stake, having put themselves on equal terms with the rest of the private Continental Circus riders. This situation proved to be the salvation of the two premier GP classes over the next few years.

Furthermore, the scarcity of works machines during the late '50s, and into the 1960s, meant that the traditional British single cylinder machines, Manx Norton, 7R AJS and G50 Matchless, once again formed the backbone of Grand Prix racing in the two premier classes, by helping to fill the grids, and even gaining some of their former prestige by achieving podium places and the occasional Grand Prix win. Apart from Surtees and Hartle, and later Hailwood and Agostini on the MVs, it was a hardcore of talented private riders, who often provided the only real interest in the two premier classes, as they battled between themselves for a possible podium place and the honour of being the first privateer behind the works machines. The usual suspects were Bob Brown, Gary Hocking, John Hartle, Mike Duff, Paddy Driver, Alan Shepherd, Frank Perris, Jack Findlay, Jack Ahearn, Phil Read, Peter Williams and Fred Stevens. They were often joined by the

Continental riders, Walter Scheimann on Nortons and Gyula Marsovsky on a Matchless G50.

Although both Norton and AMC had officially retired from Grand Prix racing, development of the production racing machines had continued under Doug Hele at Norton and Jack Williams at AMC. The Norton development machines were usually ridden by Roy Ingram, and Doug Hele also released some of the earlier works special ultra-short-stroke, 80mm bore 350, and 90mm bore 500cc engines. The 90mm bore 500cc engine had been further revised to 93x73.5mm dimensions. One of these engines was supplied to Reg Dearden for his Norton, ridden by Keith Campbell, and a similar engine went to Australian Bob Brown. An 80mm bore 350cc engine was also supplied to Geoff Duke.

At AMC, the G45 had been discontinued and development had begun on the single cylinder 78x90mm 496cc G50 Matchless, which first appeared in 1958, and was ridden in the Senior TT by Jack Ahearn. The G50 went into production in 1959, and soon proved a popular alternative to the 500 Norton. The G50 also had its share of production faults, and suffered a series of crankpin failures during 1961 and 1962, that were cured by changing the hardening process. Although it never achieved a Grand Prix win, steady development by Jack Williams, channelled through Geoff Monty, and later Tom Arter and Tom Kirby, gave the G50 its fair share of success including runner-up in the 500cc World Championships for Alan Shepherd in 1962 and 1963.

For 1958, Geoff Duke decided to build a special

The start of the 500cc Finnish GP at Helsinki in 1955.

lightweight 350 Norton, incorporating some of his personal modifications. The frame was designed and built by Ken Sprayson of Reynolds, using lightweight 531 tubing, and had a large diameter front down tube, which also acted as the engine oil reservoir. The front forks were the Reynolds leading link type. The engine which was developed by Bill Lacey had an 80mm bore, a one piece crankshaft with an outside flywheel, and an alloy connecting rod with a plain bearing big end. The cylinder head was converted to take coil valve springs. Despite its potential, this engine failed to live up to expectations, and eventually had to be abandoned due to escalating costs after a major engine blow up in the North West 200, forcing Geoff Duke to revert mostly to a standard 350 engine. Ironically, many similar engines both 80mm bore 350cc and 90mm bore 500cc, are proving to be successful in classic racing today, with the benefit of modern materials and technology.

For the 500cc class Geoff Duke had an ex-works BMW, as well as the Reg Dearden Nortons, which sometimes had one of the Norton experimental engines. Despite a win at Hockenheim on the BMW in May, Geoff Duke found the idiosyncrasies of the BMW handling, plus other minor issues, difficult to overcome, and the machine was withdrawn later in the season. This may prove the old saying that 'only Bavarians can ride BMWs.' Reverting to his Nortons, Geoff Duke scored a 350/500cc double win in the Swedish Grand Prix at Hedemora. Ex-350 World Champion Keith Campbell was back on Nortons provided by Reg Dearden. Using one of the special 93mm bore 500cc engines, he achieved a brilliant 2nd place in the 1958 500cc Belgian Grand Prix, splitting the works MVs of Surtees and Hartle. Sadly just a week later at Cadours in France, having won the 350 race, he crashed on the first lap of the 500cc race after hitting a patch of oil, and

Eric Hinton (Norton) had a 350/500 double win at St Wendel in 1957.

1957 350cc World Champion Australian Keith Campbell riding as a privateer in 1958 on his 350 Norton.

Popular 'Circus' rider Peter 'Fluebrush' Ferbrache on his AJS at Schleiz in 1959. (Courtesy Karl-Gunter Peters)

succumbed to his injuries. The crash was thought to have been caused by oil from the preceding sidecar race, and all future sidecar races were run after the solos. Keith Campbell's Moto Guzzi teammate Dickie Dale now had a Rennsport BMW, on which he had wins at the Sachsenring and Brno in August, and a 7R AJS for the 350cc class,

By now, the next wave of Commonwealth riders had started to arrive in Europe. Jim Redman and Gary Hocking from Rhodesia (Zimbabwe), Paddy Driver from South Africa, Tom Phillis from Australia, and New Zealander John Hempleman. Popular Australians Eric and Harry Hinton Junior were back with Jack Ahearn, who was riding a 7R AJS and G50 on loan from AMC. The Commonwealth contingent were joined by the usual British privateers, Dave Chadwick, Bob Anderson, Frank Perris, Peter Ferbrache and Irish riders Bob Mathews and Austin Carson. Unfortunately, Austin was another fatality when he crashed during the 350 race at Falkenberg in Sweden in 1958, having previously had some well deserved wins in Finland and Sweden, including a double win at Turku.

The Hinton brothers were always a force to be reckoned with, and Eric in particular was very successful on the Continental short circuits. He had a 500cc win at St Wendel, and a 350/500 double win at Villefranche in 1958, while Harry Junior came 2nd in the 500 race, and won the 500cc Czech GP at Brno in 1959. Eric had also inherited has father's technical expertise, and was often called upon to sort out problems with his fellow riders' machines. Many a Manx Norton would be running as sweetly as ever after his attention. Unfortunately, Harry Junior crashed during the 500cc race at Imola in 1959 and although not seriously injured, he contracted a fatal attack of pneumonia while in hospital.

Having secured a ride on Reg Dearden Nortons in 1958, Gary Hocking soon established his reputation with a brilliant ride in the German GP at the Nürburgring. Having crashed his own Norton during practice, he borrowed Jack Brett's Norton, and proceeded to harry Surtees and Hartle on the MVs, and eventually finished 3rd. Another 'water

Paddock group at the Sachsenring in 1958: privateers Gary Hocking (Norton) #8, Dickie Dale (BMW) #11, Ernst Hiller (BMW), and Jim Redman (Norton) #7.

baby,' Dave Chadwick, put up a fine performance in a cold wet 350cc race, when he finished 3rd behind the two MV riders. Newcomers Tom Phillis, Paddy Driver and John Hempleman were among the other successful Commonwealth riders. Another successful British Continental Circus exponent was Peter Ferbrache, an ex-RAF rear gunner, who sported a large curly moustache that had earned him the nickname of 'Flue-brush.' Riding 350 AJS and 500 Norton, Peter had a 500cc win at Tampere in Finland, and a 350/500 double win at Lennatin, also in Finland.

In 1959, Gary Hocking was the most successful privateer in the Continental Circus. Riding Reg Dearden Nortons, he had 350/500cc double wins at St Wendel, Zandvoort, the Gellerasloppet in Sweden, and the Eifelrennen at the Nürburgring.

Later in the year he also started riding 125 and 250cc works MZs, on which he proceeded to give MV ace Carlo Ubbiali a hard time, winning the 250cc Swedish GP, and the non-championship East German GP at the Sachsenring in August. Another double race winner was Peter Ferbrache at Helsinki in May.

After a brief flirtation with Formula One in 1958, driving a 250F Maserati, Australian Ken Kavanagh returned to two wheels and the Continental Circus, with an ex-works 125 Ducati and a pair of Nortons that were looked after by Eric Hinton. He was relatively unsuccessful, however, with one win on the Ducati, and a 4th in the 350cc and 2nd in the 500cc races at Helsinki in May. Among the other race winners in 1959 were Circus regulars, Geoff Duke, Tom Phillis, Ralph Rensen, Bob Brown, John

The immaculate Bob Brown (Norton) who was 3rd in the 500cc World Championship in 1959, and posthumously took 4th place in 1960.

Hempleman, Paddy Driver, Jim Redman, Peter Ferbrache, and Eric Hinton. There was another fatality in June, when the well know British rider John Clark, from Portsmouth, was killed after colliding with another rider at Moulins.

Riding his immaculate white, Peel-faired Nortons, partly sponsored by Geoff Duke, the stylish Bob Brown was also 3rd in the 1959 350 and 500cc World Championships. On the 350 Norton he was 3rd in the Swedish GP, 2nd in the Ulster, and 3rd in the Italian. On the 500 Norton he was 3rd in the Senior TT, using one of the ex-works 93 bore engines, and was 3rd again in the German GP. His best ride was in the 500cc Dutch TT when he finished 2nd, splitting the MVs of Surtees and Venturi.

Fred Stevens (Matchless) and Walter Scheimann (Norton) at Tubbergen in 1964. (Courtesy Karl-Heinz Reiger)

Chapter 9

THE JAPANESE INFLUENCE

The arrival of the Japanese Honda team at the TT in 1959 had been an omen for the future. Honda returned in full force in 1960, and were soon followed by Suzuki and Yamaha. The Japanese factories undoubtedly helped to revitalise World Championship Grand Prix racing, and changes began to take place which ultimately improved the sport in many ways. Eager for success, the Japanese factories began to invest heavily in experienced and successful western riders. Having signed lucrative contracts with European petrol and oil companies, they were helped in their search for new riders by the influential trade representatives. This situation proved fortunate for many regular Circus riders who secured contracts to ride for one of the Japanese factory teams

New Zealander John Hempleman, also known as 'Hempo,' who had been very successful in 1959 riding his Nortons, took Gary Hocking's place in the MZ team for 1960. He won the 250cc race at the non-championship East German GP

Popular Czech, Frankie Stastny (Jawa) in the Dutch TT in 1963. (Courtesy Malcolm Carling)

at the Sachsenring, was 3rd in the 350 race and won the 500cc race on his Nortons. He also had a 350/500cc double win on his Nortons at Schleiz in East Germany. In the classic GPs, he and his MZ team-mate, Ernst Degner, trounced the MV team in the Belgian GP on the ultra fast Spa Francorchamps circuit, with Degner setting a new record race speed, and Hempleman a new lap record at 101.91mph (164.11km/h). Gary Hocking, who had been riding MZs in 1959, had posed a serious threat to MV supremacy and was eventually poached by them for 1960, but MV obviously failed to recognise the possibility of serious rivalry between the reigning world champion Ubbiali, and the success-hungry Hocking. 1960 also saw the arrival in Europe of future world champion, New Zealander Hugh Anderson, who made his Continental debut by winning the 500 race at Madrid on his Norton. For his first TT, he was provided with a brand new

Start of the 125 race at St Wendel in 1960. Werner Musiol (MZ) #157, Dave Chadwick (MZ) #51, Ernst Degner (MZ) #156, and Jim Redman (Ducati) #165. (Courtesy Karl-Gunter Peters)

7R AJS by New Zealand dealer Percy Coleman. Riding the 7R and his 500 Norton, he began to establish his reputation during 1960, with a fine 3rd place in the 350cc Ulster GP, behind the MVs of Surtees and Hartle.

Unfortunately for the privateers, the Czech riders Frantisek (Frankie) Stastny and Gustav Havel started to appear on the Continent, with the somewhat functional looking 350cc twin cylinder Jawa machines, that often proved more than a match for the traditional Manx Norton and 7R AJS. At the age of 33 in 1960, Frankie was something of a veteran, having been a test rider for Jawa since the early 1950s. His equally capable team-mate Havel, was also employed by the Jawa factory. Stastny demonstrated the potential of the Jawa with a 350cc win in the non-championship Austrian GP, on the Salzburg autobahn circuit, and a 250/350cc double win in the Czech GP at Brno. In the classic GPs, he was 2nd to Gary Hocking's MV in the French GP, and 2nd again in the Italian GP, taking 4th place in the 350cc World Championships.

Well known Manchester rider, Dave Chadwick, had signed up to ride works MZs in 1960, while continuing to ride his private Nortons. He had a good start to the season, winning the 500cc race at the Austrian GP in May, but just a fortnight later he was killed at Mettet in a tragic accident. While leading the 500cc race on the last lap, he collided with lapped rider Bill Sawford and was forced to take to the grass verge, but struck a pie salesman who was illegally on the circuit. He was thrown off, hitting a telegraph post, and died instantly. Bill Sawford was also killed. The Belgian Federation were severely criticised for their lack of crowd control, but no further action was taken.

Peter Ferbrache from Enfield in Middlesex always seemed to be successful in Scandinavia. Having changed his 500 Norton for a G50 Matchless, he had a successful start to the season with 350/500 double wins at Ruissalon and Karlskoga. During the 350cc Dutch TT at Assen, he was involved in a battle with Bob Anderson, Paddy Driver and John Hempleman, when he crashed and received

New Zealander John Hempleman (MZ) at the Sachsenring in 1960. (Courtesy Elwyn Roberts)

Another New Zealander, Peter Pawson (Norton) in the Schauinsland Hill Climb in 1960.

head injuries to which he later succumbed. Peter 'Flue-brush' was one of the real characters of the Continental Circus and was sadly missed.

The 1960 German Grand Prix, run on the Solitude circuit near Stuttgart, was somewhat inadvisedly combined with a Formula 2 race for cars. During practice there had been several crashes in the twisty Mahdental section, allegedly caused by sand and grit brought onto the circuit by the cars. The most serious incident involved Bob Brown, who slid off his works 250 Honda at the notorious 'sand pit' corner, and received serious head injuries. He was attended to on the spot by fellow rider John Hempleman, but died in hospital later the same

Team-mate to Stastny, Gustav Havel (Jawa) at the Sachsenring in 1964. (Courtesy Elwyn Roberts)

evening. Sadly, Bob had only recently married his girlfriend Geraldine Somerville. Despite the tragedy, Bob was still the highest placed 'privateer,' with 4th place in the 500cc World Championships, behind three works MVs.

With the benefit of hindsight, it would be easy to speculate that many of these fatal head injuries could have been avoided, had the riders been wearing modern full-face helmets. Rider protection in those days consisted of almost skin-tight, one-piece leathers, with a bit of extra padding on shoulders and elbows, and the traditional 'pudding basin' helmet, basically a cork shell. Circuit safety and medical facilities were often rudimentary, particularly at some of the minor, less well known circuits. Two casualties of these poor facilities were South African rider Eddie Grant, who crashed at Villefranche de Rouergue in 1956, and although not seriously injured, was left to lie in a field until the race finished, and later died of shock and exposure, and Italian MV rider, Roberto Colombo, who crashed during practice for the Belgian GP at Spa Francorchamps, and lay in a field for several hours in blazing sunshine, until medical assistance arrived, by which time he had succumbed to his injuries. Moto GP riders today who enjoy such excellent facilities, have the pioneer Continental Circus riders to thank, for their tireless efforts to improve track safety, which often fell on deaf ears.

Race transport had also changed, and the ubiquitous Ford Thames van had now replaced most of the ex-WD vehicles, becoming the most commonly used form of transport. Some of them were fitted with Ford Zephyr engines which gave them a much higher cruising speed on autobahns and motorways, making travel between race circuits far less arduous. A few other unique forms of transport appeared, such as the Jaguar saloon with the rear bodywork chopped off and replaced with a pickup body, as used by Ian Burne, which could carry a couple of race machines, and was later acquired by Paddy and Janet Driver, while Keith Campbell used a large trailer capable of carrying as many as five bikes hitched to his Cadillac.

Gustav Havel (Jawa) leading Denis Fry (Norton) #21 and Jack Findlay #22 (Kirby Matchless) in the 1964 Dutch TT. (Courtesy Malcolm Carling)

Chapter 10

EARNING START MONEY

The need to generate as much start money as possible sometimes led the privateers to carry out mild acts of deception. A rider who had blown up his 350 Norton or 7R AJS, would swap the tank, fairing and exhaust system with the bigger machine, and start the 350cc race. Alternatively, smaller capacity machines, such as a 125 Bultaco, could be ridden in 250 classes, simply by changing the fairing bearing the appropriate colour number plates, purely to qualify for start money. However, it was an unwritten law that no rider would use such tactics to gain an unfair advantage over his friends and rivals: the usual practice was for the rider in question to retire after a few laps. It was not unknown for a rider to make a token start with a blown-up engine with a rag wrapped round the gudgeon pin, only to retire immediately. Nobby Clark recalled one amusing instance:

"A certain rider, who will remain nameless, had blown up his 7R AJS, and, in the usual manner, went out in the 350 race on his disguised G50, and continued to circulate rapidly among the rather surprised front runners for several laps, before finally retiring. At this particular meeting there was an award for the fastest lap, which, ironically, went to the rider on the illegal machine. Australian Jack Ahearn, who was a typical no-nonsense type of person, had figured out what went on in the 350 race, and advised the rider in question to hand over the award to the next fastest rider in the 350 race, which he duly did with good grace."

This perfectly illustrates the understanding that existed between the privateers.

On the subject of consolidating start money, the late Keith Campbell had always recommended ignoring the classic GPs, in favour of some of the smaller non-championship events which often paid out better start money to privateers than some GP organisers. For example, Mike Duff was paid 600DM for two starts at St Wendel in 1962, and some of the other German meetings paid around 500DM at least. Furthermore, these events did not always attract the marauding 'works' riders. Lewis Young, a long term Continental Circus privateer, tended to follow this advice. "We would go to some of the races in the East, like Portoroz and Piestany, where the pickings were often much easier. Some of these circuits, however, were very rough, and so loose-surfaced that they were more suitable for a scrambler than my 7R or G50." It was profitable for privateers to go

Liverpudlian Circus rider Ralph Rensen (Norton) in the 1961 Senior TT.

to the occasional classic GP, however, where it was possible to stock up on free tyres, chains, plugs, and so on, that were handed out by the trade reps. Many privateers would fill up their bike tanks during these meetings which were then siphoned off into their transporters. Some ambitious riders felt that a good performance in the classic GPs could lead to an invitation to join a works team, and this sometimes proved to be the case.

Following the early promise he had shown, Hugh Anderson had several wins early in 1961, including a 350/500cc double win in the Austrian GP on the Salzburg autobahn circuit, a 500cc win at Tubbergen, and a 350cc win at St Wendel. At the TT, Shell competitions manager Lew Ellis took him to meet the Suzuki team manager, and it was arranged for him to ride Suzuki's machines in the TT, Dutch TT and Belgian GP. As history records, this led to him becoming a Suzuki works rider in 1962. Unfortunately, he crashed his 7R during the 350 Dutch TT, suffering various injuries including a cracked skull. He was taken to Assen hospital where he had to spend several weeks, during which time he was looked after by a Dutch nurse called Janny, who later became his wife.

Another regular Circus exponent worthy of mention is Liverpool rider Ralph Rensen. In 1961 Ralph had a good start to the season, with 350/500cc double wins at Pau and Bourg-en-Bresse in April on his Nortons, and a 500cc and 125cc win on a Bultaco at Chimay in May. Having finished 3rd in the Junior TT, he was engaged in a battle on the road with Tom Phillis on Doug Hele's Norton Domiracer in the Senior TT, and had just recorded his first 100mph lap, when he crashed on the 5th lap at the very fast 11th milestone, and received serious injuries caused by his broken screen which severed an artery in his neck and died almost instantly.

Canadian born Frank Perris was another well known 'privateer,' who gave up his job in the AMC drawing office to join the Continental Circus with his wife Rita. Riding his Ray Petty prepared Nortons, he had several top three places in Circus events in 1961, and in the classic GPs. His 2nd

place in the West German GP and 3rd place in the Swedish helped him to finish 3rd in the 500cc World Championships, behind the MVs of Hocking and Hailwood.

Sponsorship, such as it was in the '50s and early '60s, came only from within the motorcycle industry. In addition to the financial assistance from the fuel and oil companies and the accessory manufacturers, racing dealers often provided machines for well known riders. Tom Arter's machines were ridden by Hugh Anderson, and later, Mike Duff. Tom Kirby provided bikes for Paddy Driver and Phil Read. Other well known dealers who supported riders were, Geoff Monty, Alan Dudley-Ward, Reg Dearden, George Leigh and Ray Cowles to name a few.

There is no doubt that the arrival of the Japanese factories helped to raise the standard of motorcycle racing across the board. Riders lucky enough to sign contracts with the Japanese teams were now able to improve their travel and living standards. By 1962 the use of caravans had become popular, as riders began to enjoy the obvious advantages of separate living accommodation. Some of the first privateers to use caravans were Jim Redman and Dan Shorey. However, as Dan Shorey pointed out, caravans were not allowed into Eastern Europe until after 1962, probably to thwart any attempt to smuggle people out. Hotels, too, were now used more frequently. Massive transporters, however, were still in the future, and even the Honda team used a couple of small Nissan vans in which to transport their machines and technicians.

To the dismay of the less fortunate privateers, some of the works riders such as Jim Redman and Tom Phillis had works machines for their private use, on which they often turned up at non-championship events, and obviously gave them an advantage over the private riders, particularly in the 125 and 250cc classes. Many of the National Italian meetings also attracted riders like Silvio Grassetti, and Ernesto Brambilla on Bianchi, Alberto Pagani and Renzo Passolini and even Tarquinio Provini, riding works or semi works machines. The major threat to the privateers in the 350cc class continued to be the Jawas of Frankie Stastny and Gustav Havel.

Some of the other more popular circuits among the privateers, were St Wendel in Germany, Chimay in Belgium, Tubbergen in Holland and Salzburg in Austria. The 2.27 mile (3.63km) St Wendel public roads circuit was centred around the town and its outskirts, was short and very narrow. From the start the circuit swept downhill on a long right-hand curve, at the bottom there was a sharp left-hander under a bridge, followed by another left-hander, then uphill through a long S bend, and a short straight with a left-hand hairpin at the top, before dropping down back to the start. Sometimes referred to as the Saar Grand, it was usually organised by the enthusiastic August Balthasar, who would travel round the Continent to race meetings recruiting riders for this event with start money offers. Consequently the St

Wendel meeting became very popular because of the generous start money usually paid out to well-known riders.

Chimay near the Belgian-French border, sometimes referred to as the 'Circuit of the Borders,' situated just outside the town, was 6.73 miles (10.87km) long, and very fast with lap speeds in excess of 100mph (160km/h), with long fast straights that were hard on engines. In 1961 Ralph Rensen (Norton) won the 500cc race at an average speed of 103.08mph (164.9km/h) with a fastest lap of 105.39mph (168.62km/h). The absolute lap record for the circuit of 134.19mph (216.45km/h) was set by Barry Sheene in 1977. A shorter version of this circuit was later used for classic racing. Tubbergen was another popular Dutch circuit near the German border. It was basically a three point circuit 4 miles (6.43km) in length on country roads just outside the town, and was usually administered by the enthusiastic Pinners family.

Phil Read who rode in all four classes in 1964, on the Kirby Matchless in the Belgian GP.

The 3.12 mile (4.9km) Salzburg circuit was fairly unique, in that it used part of the uncompleted Salzburg Munich autobahn. At the start, riders raced down one side of the autobahn to a slip road, which took them down under the autobahn and up onto the opposite side. About halfway along, they dived down another exit slip road to a sharp left-hander, which took them back onto the autobahn, and then down a long straight to a tight left hairpin across the central reservation onto the other side of the autobahn. Then it was down another slip road, and another sharp left-hander, back onto the autobahn and the start and finish. All the exit slip roads had a cobbled surface which made them tricky in wet conditions. These races were usually billed as the Austrian Grand Prix, until such time as new permanent Grand Prix circuits were built.

Many riders made the long trek to Scandinavia to race at circuits such as Hedemora and Karlskoga in Sweden and Helsinki, Turku and Tampere in Finland. During the early 1960s, most of the Finnish circuits were hardly up to GP standards, and often included loose-surfaced sections. In Italy, during March and April, several meetings were run on consecutive weekends on the Adriatic coast street circuits of Rimini, Cesenatico, Riccione, and Senigallia. In the far south in Spain, apart from Montjuich Park in Barcelona, there were also race meetings in Madrid, Bilbao, and Zaragoza, usually run towards the end of the season in October. Following the Le Mans disaster in 1955, motor racing was banned in Switzerland, which led to the demise of all the Swiss race circuits. As the result of the general tightening up of circuit safety, some circuits in France and Belgium were also undoubtedly affected. However, the privateers still had a large number of circuits to choose from, depending on their budgets and how much start money they were able to negotiate with the organisers.

Chapter 11

THE NEW DECADE

During the late 1950s and early '60s 125 and 250cc production racing machines were in short supply. Most of the privateers had therefore been restricted to the 350 and 500cc classes on the classic British Nortons, G50s and 7R AJS. Dickie Dale rode a Rennsport BMW during 1958 and 1959, and there were a few more BMWs ridden by German riders, Ernst Hiller, Hans-Gunter Jaeger and Austrian Gerold Klinger. The 250cc NSU Sportmax was never available in large quantities, although Mike Hailwood, Eric Hinton, Bob Brown, and Dickie Dale did race them on the Continent during the late 1950s and early '60s. Most of the other NSUs were ridden by German riders such as Hans Baltisberger, Helmut Hallmeier, Horst Kassner, and Xavier Heiss. There were also a few private 125 MVs, 250 Guzzis and a couple of very quick 250 Adlers usually ridden by Gunter Beer, Dieter Falk and Siegfried Lohmann. Many ex-works MZs usually ended up in the hands of East European riders and often proved to be as competitive as the genuine works machines.

The first of the new lightweight machines to appear in the early 1960s was the 125cc Bultaco. The birth of the Bultaco can be traced back to the Spanish Montesa company run by Pedro Permanyer and Francisco Bultaco, who produced 125cc two-stroke racing machines which proved quite successful in Spanish events and finished 2nd, 3rd, and 4th in the 1956 125 lightweight TT. When Montesa decided to pull out of racing for economic reasons, Senor Bulto, who was a dedicated racing enthusiast and had finished 5th on a Montesa in the 1951 125 Spanish

GP, left the company in 1958 to form his own company Bultaco and began producing 125cc single cylinder, two-stroke trials and moto-cross machines. In 1960 he built a 125cc racing version that was ridden by Spanish ex-patriate Juan Garcia from Malta, who raced under the name of 'John Grace.' Encouraged by a couple of podium places at Madrid and Zaragosa, a small batch of 125cc racers were built in 1961, on which John Grace and R Quintanilla finished 5th and 6th in the Spanish GP. A machine was also provided for Dan Shorey, who dominated the British National 125cc class on it in 1961.

One other new machine was the 250cc ohv push rod Aermacchi, which appeared at the Dutch TT in 1960 ridden into 9th place by Alberto Pagani who later finished 5th in the Belgian GP. A few production models called the Ala d'Oro were produced in 1961, and works riders Alberto Pagani and Gilberto Milani began to achieve podium places on the Continent, plus the occasional win at national events.

With Germany readmitted to the FIM, the inevitable BMW sidecar domination, that would last for 19 years, began in 1954. It was only Eric Oliver's exceptional skills and Cyril Smith's dogged determination that kept their Nortons competitive until then, with the occasional use of works Norton engines and the assistance of passengers, Stan Dibben, Les Nutt and Eric Bliss. In 1953, Eric Oliver pioneered the 'kneeler' driving position with his revolutionary fully enclosed Norton Watsonian. However the streamlined outfit was only used once on the Continent in

Austrian Champion Gerold Klinger on his BMW in the 1955 German GP at Solitude. (Courtesy Karl-Heinz Reiger)

the Belgian Grand Prix, when it was discovered that it was inherently unstable at high speed. The German domination began with Willi Noll and Wiggerl Kraus on works BMWs, followed by Willi Faust, Fritz Hillebrand and Walter Schneider. Willi Faust, who was considered to be the best German sidecar driver at the time, was involved in accident while practising at Hockenheim in 1955, in which his passenger Karl Remmart was killed, and Faust received serious injuries that prematurely ended his racing career.

The Continental Circus did not attract as many Commonwealth sidecar drivers as it did solo riders, most of them were from Australia. This was understandable because sidecar drivers did not qualify for ACU grants, and had to be self financed with some assistance from local Norton dealers, motorcycle clubs, and private donors. The first Australian sidecar driver on the Continent was Bernie Mack in 1953. He had a rather frustrating season, including a crash at Solitude in June. Early in the season he was 3rd at Lyon in France, 12th in the Belgian GP with passenger Ray Kelly, and was 2nd to Jacques Drion at Vesoul on 26th July, before returning prematurely to Australia.

Bob Mitchell, who was destined to become Australia's best and most successful International sidecar driver, arrived in England with passenger Max George in 1953. He raced on the Continent

over the next three years while spending the winters in England. In his Continental debut at Pau in April, he was 6th behind a host of regular Circus drivers, and the following weekend he was 5th at Mettet once again behind Eric Oliver, Cyril Smith, Jacques Drion and Julienne Deronne, but in front of Fritz Hillebrand on a BMW.

Over the next three years Bob recorded several top six places, as well as 2nd places at Mettet, Mulhouse and Lyon. A 3rd in the Dutch TT and a 5th in the German GP gave him 7th place in the 1955 World Championships. With a fully streamlined outfit, and new passenger Eric Bliss, they finished 4th in the World Championships in 1956, with 3rd in Belgium, and 4th in the Isle of Man and the Dutch TT. Eric Oliver was very impressed with Bob, and so was BMW, which offered to provide him with a machine for 1957, but later decided to withdraw from racing at the end of 1956. Bitterly disappointed, Bob decided to pack up and return to Australia with his English wife Gwen, who he had met during a visit to Norton Motors in 1954.

Two other Commonwealth sidecar drivers worthy of mention are Lindsay Urquhart and Ray Foster. Lindsay raced on the Continent in 1959 with the usual Norton outfit, and Ray Foster as passenger. Some of the highlights of Lindsay Urquhart's season were a 4th at Mettet in May, sandwiched between the BMWs of Fath, Kolle, Butscher, Neusner, and Rogliardo. A week later he was 2nd to Scheidegger at Zandvoort. At the Nürburgring Eifelrennen in July he was 4th behind the BMWs of Camathias, Scheidegger and Fath. After Lindsay Urquhart returned to Australia at the end of 1959, Ray Foster and his wife Jean stayed on, and bought a Norton outfit in 1960. Ray went racing with Jean, who joined the elite list of international lady sidecar passengers. Despite the almost overwhelming BMW domination at the time, Ray and Jean were successful enough to earn sufficient start money to keep racing in Europe until the end of 1963, before returning to Australia.

Despite the presence of the Japanese works teams and Italian machines such as the 350 Bianchi, the privateers, mainly on the British single cylinder machines, still achieved their fair share of success on the Continent in 1962. Paddy Driver and Jack Findlay on Nortons were first and second, respectively, in the 350 and 500cc races at Pau in April, Jack Findlay had a 350/500 double win at Chimay, and Mike Duff had a double win in the Eifelrennen at the Nürburgring in May.

EMC guru Dr Joe Ehrlich had obtained an MZ engine from Walter Kaaden, allegedly in exchange for a pair of Manx Norton Road Holder forks. This engine formed the basis of the new 125cc EMC that was built at the de Havilland aircraft factory where Dr Ehrlich was employed. The new EMCs proved to be quite successful in 1961 and 1962, ridden by Mike Hailwood, Phil Read, Paddy Driver, and development rider Rex Avery, who was also an employee at de Havilland. In addition to a couple

of podium places behind the works Hondas in the classic GPs in 1962, Mike Hailwood, Rex Avery and Paddy Driver took top three places at St Wendel in May.

1962 also saw the first appearance of the Russian 250 and 350cc machines in some continental events, ridden by 33-year-old Red Army Officer Nikolai Sevostianov from Moscow, and Estonian Endel Kiisa. The Russian riders were very enthusiastic, but their sometimes aggressive riding did not go down too well with some of the regular circus riders. Sometimes referred to as CKEB, the Russian Central Construction and Experimental Bureau, the 250cc S259 and 350cc S360 were both twin-cylinder double overhead camshaft machines, that bore a strong resemblance to the Jawas, which is not surprising because they were built in collaboration with the Jawa factory. Sevostianov scored World Championship points in the East German GP, with 5th place in the 250cc race and 6th place in the 350cc race.

In 1963, Honda began exporting the 125cc twin cylinder CR93 production racer, that proved a popular alternative to the 125 Bultaco, both in the UK and on the Continent. Burly Bill Smith, who was probably not ideally suited to a 125cc machine, had a win on a CR93 at Bourg-en-Bresse that year. Some of the successful Continental CR93 exponents were Walter Scheimann, Giuseppe Visenzi, Cees Van Dongen and Roland Foll. Scheimann had wins at Tubbergen in 1964 and Mettet in 1966. Visenzi was 2nd at Tubbergen and Vallelunga in 1964, and had a win

Rex Avery (EMC) in the Dutch TT 1964.

New Zealander Morrie Low, who rode Bultacos and Nortons on the Continent, is seen here on a Bultaco in the 1963 TT.

Russian ace Nikolai Sevostianov on a 350cc S360 in the 1963 Belgian GP. (Courtesy Elwyn Roberts)

at Tubbergen in 1965. The tiny wristwatch-like four-stroke Honda engines proved very reliable, but were probably slightly more complicated to maintain than the rival single cylinder two-stroke Bultacos.

Over the next few years, the new 250cc production machines, like the Bultaco and Aermacchi, began to take over from the now ageing Sportmax NSUs. Following the success of the 200cc Bultaco ridden by Dan Shorey in British national events in 1962, a full 250cc version was produced in 1963. The simple, easy to maintain, single-cylinder two-stroke soon became popular among Circus riders as a means of supplementing their 350 and 500cc rides. One of the first Bultaco Circus exponents was Ginger Molloy, followed by Jack Findlay, Morrie Low, Ralph Rensen, Gyula Marsovsky, and others.

Manx Norton production had virtually come to an end in 1961, with a few machines made in 1962 from existing spares stocks. Norton was eventually taken over by AMC in July 1962, and production of G50s and 7R AJS ended in 1963. Helping to keep the British single cylinder machines competitive were Norton engine specialists Francis Beart, Steve Lancefield, Ray Petty, and Bill Lacey. The classic singles also benefitted from updated components such as Oldani front brakes, and five- and six-speed gearboxes. Tom Phillis was one of the first to use a Swedish-made Torsten Aagard five-speed gearbox with external linkage on his Norton. The Austrian engineer Michael Schafleitner produced a neater, all-enclosed, six-speed gearbox, first used by Rudi Thalhammer and Bert Schneider on their Nortons, to win the 500cc and 350cc races at Le Mans in April 1962. Schneider and Thalhammer were also 2nd and 3rd to Mike Hailwood in the Austrian GP.

At the end of 1962, Australian Jack Findlay acquired the late Bob McIntyre's G50 Matchless special, and renamed it the 'McIntyre Matchless.' Over the next six years he became one of the most successful privateers on the Continental Circus. Based in France and riding under a French licence, Jack and his French partner, Nanou

Alan Shepherd, who rode works MZs, also rode his Matchless on which he was 2nd in the 500cc World Championship in 1962 and 1963.

Long term Circus rider Jack Findlay on the McIntyre Matchless at the Sachsenring in 1964. (Courtesy Elwyn Roberts)

Lyonnard, were very popular with their racing friends in the Circus paddocks. Multilingual Nanou also proved very useful in communicating with foreign race organisers on behalf of the riders.

Tyre development took a step forward in 1963

with the introduction of the Dunlop 'Triangular' tyres, later known as the KR73. The tyres had a triangular profile with flatter side sections, designed to provide a larger contact area when the machines were leaned over. Some riders disliked them for their tendency to suddenly break away

Pip Harris and Ray Campbell (BMW) were 3rd in the 1965 Belgian GP. (Courtesy Malcolm Carling)

during the transition from upright to banked over. However, with Avon tyres retiring from racing, like it or not, the KR73s were universally adopted. The Triangular tyres were also probably responsible for a change in riding styles that took place about this time. Due to the increase in lean angles provided by the new tyres, riders began to shift their weight inwards on corners, either by sticking their knees out or leaning inwards, or both, while keeping the machine more upright to prevent exhaust systems and other components from grounding. This later led to the development of high level exhaust systems, pioneered by Ray Petty on Derek Minter's Nortons.

Titanium components such as connecting rods also became available, marketed by George Leigh, and used on his Nortons ridden by Fred Stevens. The advantage of some of the updated components was probably responsible for some of the speeds recorded at the TT in 1963, when Roland Foll's G50 was timed at 134.00mph (214.40km/h) and Fred Stevens Norton at 132.60mph (212.16km/h). Syd Mizen's 7R AJS recorded 126.6mph (202.56km/h) and Jack Ahearn's 350 Norton 125.4mph (200.64km/h).

Honda's expansion into the 350cc class in 1963, plus the MVs and the Jawas, had made life a bit more difficult for the privateers in the classic GPs. In the non-championship events, however, the privateers were still achieving some success.

When not riding the ex-works Gileras, John Hartle had 350/500 double wins at Bourg-en-Bresse and St Wendel, in May, on his Lancefield-tuned Nortons. Some of the other successful privateers were: Mike Duff who had double wins at Helsinki and Imatra, Fred Stevens with a double win at Zolder, and Jack Findlay who had wins at Le Mans and Chimay on the McIntyre Matchless. In the classic GPs, Alan Shepherd scored several podium places on his Kirby Matchless to finish 2nd in the 500cc World Championship. Some Circus regulars were out of action in 1963 due to crashes. Bruce Beal and Gyula Marsovsky were injured at Bourg-en-Bresse in May, with Beal suffering head injuries, while Frankie Stastny suffered a broken leg in a crash at Jičín in July.

As far as the sidecar class was concerned, not many British drivers ventured out for a full season on the Continental Circus during the 1960s. Pip Harris and Jackie Beeton, followed by Colin Seeley Chris Vincent and others, had now given in to the inevitable, and resorted to the BMW Rennsport for their occasional visits to some of the classic GPs. Frenchman Jacques Drion also switched to a BMW outfit, but sadly crashed during the Czech GP at Brno in 1958, when he and Inge Stoll were both killed.

Sidecar racing has always been very popular on the Continent, particularly among the Germans and the Swiss. Despite domination by the Deubel/Scheidegger/Camathias triumvate, German drivers George Auerbacher, Otto Kolle, Arvin Ritter, and Arsenius Butscher, as well as Swiss drivers Edgar Stub and Claude Lambert regularly gave chase.

Fritz Scheidegger and John Robinson (BMW) who won the Dutch TT in 1965. (Courtesy Malcolm Carling)

As the riders regrouped for the 1964 season, it was sad to reflect that many names would be missing. Dave Chadwick, Bob Brown and Peter Ferbrache lost in 1960, Dickie Dale and Ralph Rensen in 1961, Tom Phillis and Bob McIntyre in 1962. The 125 and 250cc classes of the World Championships, now swamped by the Honda Suzuki and Yamaha teams, were a lost cause for the privateers. Although riding works 250 Yamahas in the TT, Dutch TT and Belgian GP, Mike Duff still had to earn his living with his 7R and G50. In the 350cc class, he had a season-long battle for 2nd place in the Championship, with Bruce Beal on an ex-works twin cylinder Honda. Mike was 2nd in the Ulster GP and 3rd in the TT, West German and East German GPs, but due to the points scoring system he eventually finished 3rd in the World Championships.

In the 500cc class, 40-year-old Jack Ahearn (Norton) won his first and only GP at Imatra in Finland, which together with a 2nd place in the German GP at Solitude, and podium places in East Germany, Ulster and Italy gave him 2nd place in the 500cc World Championships. Australian veteran Jack Ahearn, who had first raced in Europe in 1954, had improved with age, together with his racing philosophy of riding – expecting to find a patch of oil round the next corner, and preserving his machines by not exceeding the recommended rev limit. Tall and well built, Jack did not suffer fools gladly, and his no-nonsense approach had earned him a great deal of respect among his

Circus regular Mike Duff on his Matchless in 1964, before being drafted into the Yamaha team in 1965. (Courtesy Malcolm Carling)

Full time Circus rider Lewis Young (Matchless) in the German GP at Solitude in 1964. (Courtesy Lewis Young)

Mike Duff rode Tom Arter's Porcupine AJS in the 1964 Belgian GP. (Courtesy Malcolm Carling)

fellow riders. Phil Read (Matchless) and Mike Duff (Matchless) were 3rd and 4th respectively in the World Championship. Jack Findlay temporarily rode a Kirby G50, while a new frame was built for the McIntyre, and a 7R engine was installed in the original frame. In the sidecar class, Colin Seeley and Wally Rawlings were 3rd in the World Championships with an excellent win in the Dutch TT, in which Chris Vincent and Keith Scott were 2nd with their BMW ahead of the usual Continental opponents, Scheidegger, Deubel and Camathias.

As described by Michelle Duff in her excellent book *Make Haste Slowly*, a typical example of the camaraderie and unselfishness that existed between the privateers was at the final round of the 500cc World Championship at Monza. A race-long battle for 3rd place raged between Jack Ahearn, Jack Findlay, Mike Duff and Gyula Marsovsky. Exiting the Parabolica on the last lap, Jack Ahearn led the charge to the finish line from Mike Duff, who drew alongside him as they approached the finish line. Mike Duff, who had nothing to gain, eased off to let Jack Ahearn take the 3rd place he needed to finish 2nd in the World Championships. History has recorded several other similar unselfish examples.

In the non-championship events, New Zealander Morrie Low had 350/500 double wins at Skofja Loka and Zolder on his Nortons. Rob Fitton (Nortons) had a 350 win at Tubbergen and was 2nd to Walter Scheiman (Norton) in the 500cc race. Trevor Barnes won the 250 race at Tubbergen on his Guzzi. Vernon Cottle also did well with 3rd places on his Nortons in the Eifelrennen, Tubbergen and Zolder. At the Eifelrennen meeting on the Nürburgring South circuit in April, Mike Duff had been engaged in a battle for the lead in the 350 race, with Rudi Thalhammer, Hein Butz and Karl Hoppe, when he crashed, sustaining concussion and a broken collar bone. After trying out Tom Arter's Porcupine AJS during practice at the Dutch TT, Mike Duff rode it in the Belgian GP where it proved to be more suitable, engaging

Colin Seeley and Wally Rawlings with the BMW/FCS in the 1964 Belgian GP. (Courtesy Malcolm Carling)

Alan Shepherd 250 (MZ) who was 3rd in the 1964 Belgian GP. (Courtesy Malcolm Carling)

Phil Read and Paddy Driver's G50s in a scrap for 3rd place, until a mechanical failure caused its retirement. There was a serious accident at the AVUS in Germany on 29th August, when Florian Camathias collided with Max Deubel and George Auerbacher. Camathias suffered concussion and his passenger Alfred Herzig lost a leg.

A new 350cc GP class contender in 1964 was the 350cc version of the Aermacchi, ridden by works riders Renzo Passolini and Gilberto Milani. Milani was 4th in the West German GP and Passolini was 4th in the Italian GP. Most of the Circus privateers, however, still remained faithful to their 350 Nortons and 7R Ajays. Mike Duff, Derek Woodman, Fred Stevens and Vernon Cottle all recorded top six finishers in the classic GPs on their 7Rs, while Jack Ahearn and Chris Conn did likewise with their Nortons. After some promising results including 6th place in the West German GP and 5th place in the East German GP on his 7R, Circus privateer 38-year-old Vernon Cottle, crashed during practice for the Finnish GP at Imatra, and received head injuries to which he succumbed.

Previously, riders of British single cylinder machines had sought to improve braking by fitting Italian Oldani front brakes. Bob McIntyre used a Gilera front brake on his lightweight 500 Norton and Alan Shepherd used an MZ front brake on his Matchless in 1962. During 1963, Daniele Fontana had fitted a modified double sided Oldani brake to the works Bianchi, ridden by Remo Venturi. This caused the Gilera and MV riders to complain about being out-braked by the Bianchi rider. In

Max Deubel and Emil Horner (BMW) leading eventual winners Fritz Scheidegger and John Robinson in the 1965 Dutch TT. (Courtesy Malcolm Carling)

1964 Fontana redesigned this brake, and started building double-sided four-leading-shoe front brakes in magnesium alloy. Jack Findlay was one of the first private riders to use this brake in the McIntyre Matchless, and it soon became popular with many riders and manufacturers including Benelli and Aermacchi. The Fontana eventually became the definitive front brake, and replicas of these brakes are still manufactured today and used on many classic racing machines.

Near the end of the 1964 season, Alan Shepherd reaped the rewards of his efforts on the MZs and his G50 Matchless, by signing a contract to ride works Hondas in 1965 and 1966. He was due to make his debut at the non-championship Japanese GP at Suzuka, but during a pre-race practice session while trying to solve a handling problem on one of the 350 fours, the machine went out of control and threw him off, causing severe head injuries that put him into a coma for a couple of weeks. Although he eventually recovered, it was the end of his GP career when the FIM refused to grant him an international licence.

Jim Redman's protégé, Bruce Beal, on an ex-works 250cc twin cylinder Honda in the 1965 Belgian GP. (Courtesy Malcolm Carling)

One story from 1964 is worthy of mention, and typifies the Continental Circus experience. It concerns Richard Morley, a qualified engineer and gearbox designer, who arranged to race 125, 250 and 256cc Moto Parilla machines supplied by the factory, through the British concessionaires, in return for the design and development of six- or seven-speed gearboxes for proposed future racing machines. At this stage Parilla machines had not achieved any real success in European racing, and by current standards were relatively uncompetitive. Having negotiated the offer of £50 start money for most meetings, Richard and his mechanic friend, Vic Wooton, set off in their Ford Thames van for a season on the Continent.

After a baptism of fire at the Eifelrennen on the daunting Nürburgring, Richard was relieved to finish 18th in the 350 race, and 20th in the 500. He also discovered that many Circus riders felt that the Nürburgring Nordschliefer circuit was hard on machines, and rode there only once a year unless they were on works machines – one of the important lessons he was to learn during the season. From the Ring, he headed due south on 3 May to St Wendel, home of the Saar Grand Prix, where he came a disappointing 14th on the 125, and 11th on the 250. The 125cc race was won by Chris Vincent, from Walter Schieman and Giuseppe Visenzi on Hondas. Ginger Molloy won the 250 race on his Bultaco, followed by Bruce Beal (Honda) and Jack Ahearn (Cotton)

Richard's first experience of Eastern Europe was at the Budapest Gold Cup races in Hungary,

Privateer Richard Morley, who rode 125, 250 and 256cc Parilla machines on the Continent in 1964.

Richard Morley on his 250cc Parilla in the 1964 Ulster GP.

for which riders had to apply for visas at the Hungarian Embassy in Vienna, before being permitted to cross the border. In those days this was one of the problems for riders wishing to race in East Germany, Czechoslovakia and Yugoslavia. While in Budapest, the riders enjoyed the luxury of the Grand Hotel, courtesy of the organisers. It was in Hungary that Richard first discovered that many riders used the local currency prize money for buying things like Leica cameras, binoculars, crystal, and such like, which they exchanged for hard currency in Vienna. This practice led to an amusing incident. When he reached the border control on the way back, a long queue had formed behind a rider at the front who had some tyres strapped to the roof of his van, which he claimed were for his personal use. The customs officials seemed unconvinced because the tyres were very clearly large tractor tyres. This was just another example of the way in which riders tried to earn some extra money to keep racing.

After Budapest came the Skofja Loka races in Slovenia, on another public roads circuit. During practice, Richard suffered his first and only crash of the season, when the 125 seized and he ended up in the front garden of a house, suffering bruises and a sprained wrist and ankle. An interesting incident on race day occurred after Ginger Molloy and other New Zealand and Australian riders were arrested, following a typical boisterous incident at a restaurant the previous evening. After negotiations between the organisers and the authorities, the riders were eventually released and allowed to race. Richard recorded his first podium finish with 3rd place in the 250 race, won by Ulf Svensson (Bultaco), with Rudi Thalhammer (Aermacchi) 2nd. The 350 race was won by Morrie Low (AJS), with John Smith (AJS) 2nd, and Eddie Lenz (Norton) 3rd.

Programme cover from St Wendel, Germany, May 3rd, 1964.

By now, Richard had become one of the regulars, enjoying the friendships that usually sprang up in the race paddocks. From Yugoslavia it was on to Albi in France on 4th June, run on a two-mile airfield circuit, the original Albi road circuit having been discontinued. Richard had to be content with 11th in the 125 race, but suffered a DNF in the 250 race. The 125 race was won by Ulf Svensson (Honda) with J-P Beltoise and Jess Thomas, on Bultacos, 2nd and 3rd. Ramon Torras (Bultaco) won the 250 race, followed by J-P Beltoise (Morini), and Peter Gibson (Ducati). J-P Beltoise also won the 500 race on a G50, with

South African Ian Burne (Norton) circa 1964.
(Courtesy Malcolm Carling)

Ginger Molloy (G50) 2nd, and Rob Fitton (Norton) 3rd. Richard finished 9th on his 256 Parilla.

The Schleizer Dreieck Rennen, on 14th June, was run on the 8km road circuit that was built in 1923, and was at the time the oldest race circuit then in use in Europe. It was an unfortunate fact of life, that at some race meetings, the regular Circus riders had to compete against GP riders on works machines. The entry at Schleiz included works MZs, Jawa and CZ riders, as well as the inevitable East German riders on ex-works MZs, plus Bruce Beal on a works 250 Honda four. The 125cc race was won by Jochen Leitert (MZ), followed by Hartmut Bischoff (MZ), and Bruce Beal (Honda). Dieter Krumpholz (MZ) won the 250 race from Bruce Beal (Honda), with Morrie Low (Bultaco) 3rd, and Richard Morley 4th on his Parilla.

It was not uncommon to see the two New Zealanders, Ginger Molloy and Morrie Low, mixing it with the works MZs. Richard noticed that the MZ riders, good as they were, due to their lack of regular short circuit racing, lacked some of the cut and thrust of the regular western Circus riders, and would dutifully line up on the left-hand side approach to a right-hand corner, leaving the door open for the Circus boys to rush up the inside and take the corner from them.

The next race was at Opatija which later became the Yugoslav Grand Prix circuit. It was an idyllic setting, with the paddock situated near the start line overlooking the bay with golden sandy beaches. Having arrived a week earlier and feeling bored, Lewis Young, Ramon Robinson and a few other riders started riding round the circuit. On one lap approaching the first uphill hairpin they encountered a policeman waving his hands. However, it turned out that he was only trying to stop the traffic, so that they could have a clear run through the bend. It was all great fun.

Ramon Robinson also experienced another somewhat amusing incident in the 125cc race. Having been delayed when his Bultaco flooded at the hairpin, he started going up the hill, and was confronted with the sight of riders everywhere, emerging from the bushes, trying to get their bikes back on the road. It transpired that a rider had broken his primary chain and spilled oil all over the road, causing the following riders to

Dan Shorey (Norton) braving the cobbles in the 1964 Austrian GP on the Salzburg Autobahn circuit. (Courtesy Dan Shorey)

crash. Waving to them, Ramon continued on his way.

The 250 race was won by Morrie Low (Bultaco), with Czech rider Chaluphik (Jawa) 2nd, and Les Allan 3rd, also on a Bultaco. The 350 race was won by Frantisek Srna (Jawa), followed by Nikolai Sevostianov (CKEB), and Miroslav Cada (Jawa). Opatija proved to be a very special place with glorious weather, golden sandy beaches, crystal clear sea and local restaurants offering delicious seafood dishes at extremely low prices; it was no wonder that many riders and their wives, girlfriends, and mechanics decided to linger there for several days.

Bautzen was another less well known circuit in East Germany. Titled the 'Bautzener Autobahnring Rennen,' the circuit used part of an Autobahn (as the name suggests) that was closed for racing. Being in East Germany, the MZ and Jawa works riders were out in force again. The 125 race was won by Heinz Rosner (MZ), who also won the 250 race, with team-mate Dieter Krumpholz 2nd, and Richard a well earned 4th on his Parilla.

Richard's next race in Czechoslovakia was at Pistany, a small town on the shore of a very large lake. He had experienced the usual problems with the East German border crossings, and was forced to return via the crossing by which he had entered the county. This entailed a long detour via Germany and Austria to reach Czechoslovakia. The circuit was just outside the town, and quite uninteresting, using part of a disused airfield with a very poor surface. Once again Richard had to contend with the MZ works riders in the 125 and 250 race. He retired in the 125cc race, and was 8th in the 250 race won by Klaus Enderlein, with Heinz Rosner 2nd.

The West German Grand Prix on 19th July at the 11.4km Solitude circuit, just outside Stuttgart, was Richard's first World Championship event. Many of his Circus colleagues expressed surprise that his entries had been accepted for the 125 and 250cc races. With all the works teams present, his prospects were quite daunting. This proved to be the case in 125 practising, when the works Hondas, Suzukis, and even MZs were passing him, going at least 40mph faster. Consequently he was unable to qualify for the 125 race. He did better with the 250, and

Programme cover from the German Grand Prix at Solitude, July 18-19th, 1964.

managed to tuck in behind a quick NSU through the Mahdentaal bends. Revving to 9400rpm, he pulled out of the NSU's slipstream, and was able to cross the line alongside the NSU to eventually qualify for 5th row on the grid. As far as the regular Circus riders were concerned, Mike Duff and Paddy Driver had a good scrap for 3rd place, with Gilberto Milani's works Aermacchi, and Mike Duff eventually getting the podium finish.

During practice Richard was able to take advantage of his pre-season arrangement with Dunlop to supply him with new tyres at GPs, and any other International meeting it supported. This was fairly common practice among Circus riders, who had contracts for fuel, oil, sparkplugs, chains, and other accessories, together with bonus payments for particularly good results. This was an important lifeline, that helped most Circus riders to continue racing during the season. Unfortunately, Richard suffered a mechanical problem near the end of the 250 race, and only just managed to make it to the finish, failing to qualify for a finisher's award. Examination of the engine revealed big end failure. This led to a story that is fairly typical of the Continental Circus.

The following episode clearly illustrated the kindness and generosity of strangers when involved in the sport of motorcycle racing. Parked next to Richard in the Solitude paddock was a German rider with two immaculate Manx Nortons, who came over to enquire about the problem with the Parilla, which was now in need of a new big end. The German rider, whose name was Albert, said he knew of an engineering firm that would turn out a new crankpin. The next morning

Albert took Richard and his mechanic, Vic, to an upmarket precision engineering company, a subsidiary of Heinkel, near Stuttgart. Albert evidently had some influence here, and, after a meeting with the company directors, the crankcase assembly was taken to an immaculate workshop, where the chief engineer said he would strip the crankcases and make a new crankpin by the following day.

After spending the rest of the day with Albert's family, who lived in a very affluent part of Augsburg, Richard and Vic arrived at the workshop

Programme from the East German Grand Prix at Sachsenring, July 25-26th, 1964.

the next morning, to find the crankcases had already been reassembled and cleaned down ready to go back into the frame. With just two days left before the East German GP, Richard and Vic thanked Albert and the chief engineer profusely, before setting off for the Sachsenring. About three months later Richard received the sad news that Albert Achinger, age 24, the rider who had helped him in Germany, had been killed on 30th August while riding his 500 Norton at the AVUS circuit. Although their paths had crossed just briefly, the memory of Albert's kindness remains with Richard and Vic.

Despite its performance limitations, Richard qualified his Parillas for all three classes 125, 250, and 350, of the East German GP on 25/26th July, but was later taken off the 250 start list on the grounds that he would have exceeded the maximum mileage rule. However, the real reason was that MZ had additionally entered Mike Hailwood for the 250 race, and needed the entry. However the organisers agreed to pay Richard's agreed start money for all three races because he had qualified. The money was split between East Germany currency and Deutsch Marks. 100/150DM for the 125, 125/200DM for the 250 and 150/250DM for the 350. After a close encounter with Luigi Taveri, while being lapped in the 125 race, when Luigi missed a gear coming out of a corner, Richard finished 20th, gaining his first World Championship finisher's medal, but clutch problems forced him to retire in the 350 race. Mike Duff, who was engaged in a battle with Bruce Beal's Honda for 2nd place in the Championship, came 3rd, with Beal 4th, followed by Vernon Cottle and Fred Stevens 5th and 6th on their AJS 7Rs.

From East Germany Richard faced the long trek across Europe and England to Dundrod in Ireland, for his third and final World Championship GP. Despite the inevitable rains, he finished 10th in the 125 race, 13th in the 250 race, but had to retire in the 350 race due to cramp. For his efforts, together with the start money for all three races, he also won the 250cc Private Entrants Handicap

South African Paddy Driver was another Circus regular, on his Kirby AJS at the Sachsenring in 1964. (Courtesy Elwyn Roberts)

award. It was then off to Spain for the usual end of season Circus events.

The Spanish series started at Bilbao on August 30th, followed by races at Valladolid, Jerez and Barcelona, ending in Madrid on 14th October. The Bilbao circuit, de Begoña, was approximately two miles long, consisting of both sides of a public dual carriageway with hairpin bends at both ends. With the races restricted to 125 and 250cc machines, the opposition consisted of Circus regulars Ramon Robinson, Barry Smith, Andy Rickman and American Jess Thomas, plus the inevitable quick local riders on Spanish-built Bultaco, Ducati, Montesa, Ossa, and so on. Fortunately, the Japanese and Italian works teams were occupied elsewhere. On arrival in the Paddock a few days before official practice, Richard received the sad news that New Zealander Morrie Low had been killed while riding in the Freiberg Hillclimb in Germany. This came as a great shock, because Morrie was one of those very fast, but smooth, riders who never looked to be riding near the ragged edge.

After being struck down by the 'Spanish Lurgy,' Richard missed the first practice session. But as Ramon Robinson later recalled, he was lucky: "After a long dry spell a shower of rain fell just before the first practice session, making the oil soaked tarmac extremely slippery. Having been warned, I took it easy down to the first hairpin to find the road littered with fallen bikes and riders." Despite the after-effects of his stomach bug, Richard was pleased to finish 3rd in the 125 race, won by Ramon Torras, with Jess Thomas 2nd, and was 6th in the 250 race – no doubt helped by several over-enthusiastic riders who fell off at the hairpin bends.

In another example of the kindness shown to visiting Circus riders, while he was ill, Richard had been looked after for three days by a Spanish family, who refused to accept any financial contribution for their hospitality and generosity.

As often happens, Richard and his fellow racers; Ramon Robinson, Andy Rickman, and Barry Smith decided to travel in company for the rest of the races in Spain. Ramon Robinson rode a 125 Bultaco, and shared a 250 Parilla with his travelling companion Andy Rickman. He also spoke fluent Spanish, and was appointed spokesman for the group when dealing with organisers, ordering meals, and asking for directions.

Valladolid was another typical urban street circuit in the middle of the town. The 125 race was won by Ramon Torras (Bultaco), with Cesar Garcia (Lube-Renn) 2nd, and Richard 3rd on his Parilla. The 250 race was won by Franco Farne (Ducati), after

a last corner incident with race leader Barry Smith (Aermacchi), who eventually finished 2nd, with Richard 3rd again on the Parilla. During the races, the crowds had inevitably pushed past the barriers and onto the track, often leaving only a narrow racing line.

The Jerez circuit, La Constancia, was very similar to the Valladolid circuit, featuring another dual

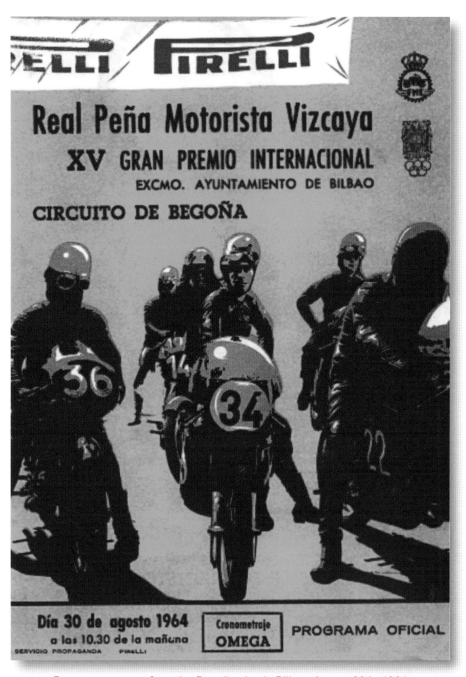

Programme cover from the Begoña circuit, Bilbao, August 30th, 1964.

carriageway joined to a small section round a block of buildings and a street market, before rejoining the dual carriageway. Like Bilbao and Valladolid, the races were run anti-clockwise. Starting from the front row of the 125 race, surrounded by Spanish riders, Richard had a battle with Ramiro Blanco (Bultaco) for 3rd place, and his 3rd podium finish. The race was won again by Ramon Torras, with Cesar Garcia 2nd. Ramon Torras also won the 250 race, with Barry Smith (Aermacchi) 2nd, Ramon Millet (Montesa) 3rd, Chris Goosen (Bultaco) 4th, and Richard 5th. Once again, the enthusiastic spectators had pushed past the rope and straw bale barriers, and were sitting and standing on the track. Inevitably, a Spanish rider crashed, injuring himself and a number of spectators when his bike went off the circuit.

On arrival at Montjuich, several riders found their entries had not been accepted. The meeting was heavily oversubscribed with priority having been given to the Spanish works entries. The races were to be run over a shortened section of the original circuit, joined at both ends by inner link roads within the park, that included a long downhill left-hand curve with a very bumpy surface. Richard had only been accepted for the 125 race in which he retired, the race being won by Ramon Torras (Bultaco).

The final meeting in Madrid was held on the 'Parc de Ritero' circuit that surrounded a large lake close to the city. The most distinguishing feature of the circuit was a long sweeping left-hander connecting the two main straights together. The surface of this corner was like polished marble, and had to be treated with caution. In spite of a good start in the 250 race, Richard was unable to stay with the leading Spanish riders, who soon pulled away. About halfway through the race, he was passed by Barry Smith on his Aermacchi, and was able to get a tow past several riders up to 7th place. The race was won by Jose Busquets (Montesa), followed by Renzo Passolini (Aermacchi), and Pedro Millet (Montesa). Taking stock at the end of the season Richard had entered 38 races spread across 7 countries, including 3 World Championship meetings, in what had been a fairly typical racing year for the average Circus rider.

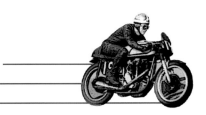

By 1965, many of the former Commonwealth privateers such as Jim Redman, Hugh Anderson and Mike Duff, were now fully occupied as works riders for Honda, Suzuki and Yamaha. Phil Read and Frank Perris had given up their British singles to concentrate on their respective works rides with Yamaha and Suzuki. However, this did not make it any easier for the Circus privateers, who had to contend with works riders on works machines turning up at the non-championship meetings.

At Imola, Jack Ahearn was 4th in the 500 race. In the Austrian GP on the Salzburg autobahn circuit, Dan Shorey (Norton) won the 500 race, Chris Conn (Norton) was 2nd, and Billie Nelson (Norton) 4th. Jack Ahearn (Norton) was 2nd in the 350 race, followed by Ron Robinson and Dan Shorey. Trevor Barnes was 4th in the 250 race on his Guzzi. Dan Shorey said the Salzburg Cobblestone corners were okay if dry, but in the wet they were a nightmare, though this did not seem to bother the East German riders.

Ginger Molloy did well at Bourg-en-Bresse, winning the 250 race on his Bultaco, and the 500 race on a Norton, while John Smith (Norton) won the 350 race from Robin Fitton. At Tubbergen in June, Robb Fitton won the 350 race, Trevor Barnes was 3rd in the 250, and 4th in the 350 on his Guzzis. John Smith won the 500 on a Norton, followed by Eddie Lenz and Ginger Molloy (Nortons), and Colin Burton (G50). The meeting was marred by the death of John Bacon who was riding his 250 Greeves.

Dan Shorey won the 350 race at Zolder in July, with Chris Conn 2nd, and Hungarian expatriate

Programme cover from Circuit Tubbergen, June 7th 1965.

Gyula Marsovsky (then living in Switzerland) won the 500 race on his Matchless from Shorey and Fred Stevens. At Zaragoza in October, Marsovsky won the 500 race from Jack Findlay and Dan Shorey.

The situation in the 500cc class was less desperate for the privateers, with only the two

John Cooper (Norton) who was 4th in the 1965 Dutch TT following arch rival Derek Minter (Norton). (Courtesy Malcolm Carling)

MVs of Hailwood and Agostini ranged against a horde of Manx Nortons and G50 Matchless. Paddy Driver was 3rd in the 500cc World Championships on his Tom Kirby G50, with podium places in the Dutch TT, East German GP, the Ulster and the Finnish GP, after some closely fought battles with Fred Stevens on his G50, who finished 4th in the Championship. In Czechoslovakia it was Jack Ahearn's turn to harry Driver, with the Australian beating the South African by half a length to take 3rd spot.

One of the most exciting privateer battles of the season was in the 500cc

Dan Shorey (Norton) followed by Jack Findlay (McIntyre) and Mike Duff (Matchless) at the Sachsenring in 1965.

Belgian GP in which, Paddy Driver, Fred Stevens and Gyula Marsovsky on G50s were locked in combat for most of the race with Derek Minter, Chris Conn, and South African Ian Burne on Nortons. In the closing stages, Minter and Driver managed to break away to finish 3rd and 4th, while the other four, led by Fred Stevens, were covered by less than two seconds at the finish.

The Dutch TT programme cover from June 26th, 1965.

The 1966 Continental season started on a tragic note, when Manxman Syd Mizen was killed at Le Mans on April 3rd. Having finished 4th in the 350 race on his 7R, in the 500 race he ran into the back of Bill Smith's G50, when it seized on the Mulsanne straight. Rob Fitton won the 350 and 500 races on his Nortons, Rod Gould was 2nd in the 350 and 3rd in the 500, and Marsovsky was 2nd in the 500 on his G50.

The race meeting on the Italian Cervia street circuit on April 10th was abandoned after the 125 and 250 races, when heavy rain made the already slippery surface treacherous, causing crashes in which Agostini, Remo Venturi and Giuseppe Mandolini were injured.

At Imola on April 17th, John Cooper (Norton) was 3rd in the 500cc race behind Agostini's MV, and Derek Minter's Gilera. Stuart Graham, son of 1949 World Champion Les Graham, in his first full-time year on the Continent, was 4th on his Jim Ball-sponsored G50, and Jack Ahearn was 5th on his Norton.

In the 125cc class the Honda CR93 Circus riders now faced some opposition from Australian

Stuart Graham was a brilliant 2nd in the wet 1966 Belgian GP. He is seen here on his Matchless in the 1963 Senior TT. (Courtesy Malcolm Carling)

Ken Carruthers on his Gates Honda, allegedly an ex-works machine with a six speed gearbox. Circus newcomer, Jim Curry, who was sponsored by Ralph Varden on a CR93, also had the ex-Ron Pladdys 182cc CR93 for the 250cc class. Their closest Honda rival was the German rider Walter Scheimann, the three of them were often involved in close fought battles. There were also the inevitable ex-works 125 and 250cc MZs, that were usually handed down to East German riders through their local motorcycle club.

The introduction of the 250cc water-cooled TSS Bultaco had provided some of the hard-pressed privateers with a money-earning 250cc machine. Among them were Jack Findlay, who had sold the 350 McIntyre to Brian Ball, Ginger Molloy, Gyula Marsovsky and Eric Hinton. Jack Findlay was the most successful in 1966, with a wins at Mettet and Chimay, plus several top six places in the classic

Jim Curry (Honda) on the Salzburg Austrian GP cobbles in 1966. (Courtesy Jarda Sejk)

GPs which earned him 7th place in the 250cc World Championships. Ginger Molloy won the 250 Ulster, following the retirement of the Japanese works teams, with Marsovsky 2nd, and Kevin Cass 3rd, also on Bultacos.

At the traditional Eifelrennen meeting on April 24th. The 350 race was won by M Zeller on a 7R from Karl Hoppe, also on a 7R, and Billie Nelson was 3rd on his Norton. Karl Hoppe won the 500 race on a G50, Walter Scheimann was 2nd on a Norton, with Billie Nelson taking his second podium in 3rd place. In his Circus debut, Jim Curry was 5th in the 125 race, after a race-long battle with Walter Scheimann who pipped him for 4th place behind the works Hondas and Suzukis.

Most of the Circus boys headed for Salzburg from Germany, for the usual battle with the cobbles on the Autobahn circuit. Jack Findlay (McIntyre Matchless) won the 500 race, Chris Conn was 2nd on a Kirby G50, Australian newcomer Kel Carruthers (Norton) 3rd, Lewis Young (G50) 4th, and Jack Ahearn 5th. Mike Hailwood made a brief appearance to walk away with the 350 race on his Honda. The Adriatic street circuit of Cesanatico on April 24th was dominated by works MVs, Hondas, Benellis and Aermacchis, but John Cooper was 3rd in the 350 race on his Norton, followed by Derek Minter who was now riding Seeleys. Dan Shorey was 5th on his Norton. John Cooper was 3rd again in the 500 race, with Jack Ahearn 5th, and Stuart Graham 6th.

Travel to the Eastern European circuits still presented many difficulties. Most of the roads through Czechoslovakia and East Germany were quite bad. Obtaining entry visas was quite complicated, and border crossings often took several hours while carnets and passports were scrutinised and vans searched. Many riders experienced some trepidation when entering East Germany, in particular, due to the extreme security measures in place at that time. Straying from the direct route to the circuit could have serious consequences, and exit was only permitted via the point of entry. Dan Shorey admitted that he was always extremely relieved to get out.

Swiss Hungarian Gyula Marsovsky, who was a successful Continental Circus rider, is seen here on his Matchless in the 1967 Senior TT.

Start and prize money had to be paid out in a mixture of local currency and hard currency, which encouraged the largely cash-strapped privateer riders to buy up local goods such as cameras, binoculars, and crystal glassware in Czechoslovakia, and even superbly manufactured shotguns, which were carefully hidden away in their vans to be exchanged for hard currency once back in Western Europe.

Meanwhile the privateers soldiered on in the non-championship events. Chris Conn won the 500cc race at Mettet after a race-long slipstreaming battle with Jack Ahearn, both on Nortons, with Chris timing his overtaking move to perfection to pip Jack on the line. They were followed by Walter Scheimann and Dan Shorey also on Nortons.

Next came the long, fast Chimay circuit on May 29th, prior to a meeting at Tubbergen on the 30th, where Rob Fitton (Norton) won the 500 race from Jack Findlay, with Rudi Thalhammer 3rd and Chris Conn 4th. Jack Findlay also won the 250 race on his Bultaco. Brits Barry Dungworth and Neil Caddow (BMW) followed their Mettet win, taking the sidecar race in Chimay from Siggi Schauzu with Tony Wakefield and Graham Milton finishing 3rd with their BMW.

The Chimay circuit used during the 1960s was 10.8km (6.49 miles). The start/finish was situated on a long straight, with fast left curves leading to a double right-hander. This was followed by another fast section, with some demanding left and right curves, and a quick left right bend, before turning right and heading back towards Chimay town through another fast left and right, slightly downhill, to a sharp right-hander, and then another long straight with a fast left-hander before the finish.

At Tubbergen on May 30th Eric Hinton won the 250 race on a Bultaco from Gunter Beer on an ex-works Honda twin, while Jim Curry did well to finish 4th on his 182cc CR93 Honda. Karl Hoppe won the 350 race on a 7R, with Rob Fitton 2nd, and Jack Ahearn 3rd on Nortons. Robin Fitton won the 500 race on his Norton from Ophie Howard on a Matchless. Experienced Circus campaigner Lewis Young ventured out to Opatija in Yugoslavia, where he finished 3rd in the 350 race, and was 2nd to Grassetti's Bianchi in the 500 race.

Meanwhile, others headed for Jicin in Czechoslovakia. The 14km circuit was located in the countryside on the outskirts of the town, passing through two small villages with a good mixture of fast and slow corners, including a very fast 4km stretch with some changes in elevation. A cobbled section ended with a bottom gear right-hander leading to the start and finish. The 250 race was won by Jack Findlay on his Bultaco, with Jim Curry 2nd on his 182cc CR93 Honda.

The Spa Francorchamps circuit in the Ardennes was prone to sudden thunderstorms. At the Belgian GP on July 3rd, such a storm erupted just before the start of the 500cc race, and the roads were soon awash. Many riders fell off, including Jim Redman, who broke an arm when his Honda aquaplaned on the approach to the Burneville bends, and Derek Woodman broke a leg when he crashed his new G50 Metisse. In spite of the conditions, a fierce scrap for 2nd place evolved between privateers Stuart Graham and Gyula

Marsovsky on G50s, and Jack Ahearn on his Norton. With little concern for the conditions, the three riders fought a race-long battle, with Stuart Graham, displaying all the wet weather ability that he had evidently inherited from his father, emerging the victor to take 2nd place ahead of Jack Ahearn and Gyula Marsovsky. It was no doubt this performance, plus a 4th in the West German and a 5th in the Dutch TT, that led to Stuart being drafted into the Honda team, to replace the injured Jim Redman.

After the Dutch TT and Belgian GP, the Circus arrived at Zolder on 10th July, when Marsovsky won the 250 race on his Bultaco, with Jack Findlay 2nd, and Eric Hinton (Bultaco) 3rd. Jack Findlay won the 500 race on the McIntyre and Dan Shorey was 2nd on his Norton. At the end of the season, Jack Findlay was the highest placed privateer, finishing 3rd in the 500cc World Championships on the McIntyre Matchless, with a 2nd in the East German, 3rd in Finland, and 3rd in the Italian GP, plus more top six places in the Dutch TT, Czech GP, and the Ulster.

Having reached an agreement with AMC, allowing him to build new racing machines using 7R and G50 engines, in 1966 Colin Seeley produced a new 7R and G50, using a frame of his own design, and a new British racing machine the Seeley was born. Following the collapse of the Norton Villiers group later in 1966, Colin Seeley acquired the entire stock of Manx Norton, 7R and G50 spares plus design drawings, jigs, tools and manufacturing rights which would enable him to start building Seeley machines on a small scale. The entire Norton stock was eventually sold to sidecar racer John Tickle, who later went on to produce the Manx T5 in limited numbers.

In 1967, the Continental Circus continued to attract those who wished to make a living racing motorcycles. The climate had changed slightly, and racing was becoming more expensive across the board. The G50 Matchless had taken over as the most successful 500cc privateer machine, and, together with a few Nortons, it continued to fill the top six places behind Mike Hailwood's Honda and Agostini's MV. The highest placed Norton in the World Championships was Chris Conn in 15th place, by virtue of his 5th place in the Senior TT. The Giuseppe Pattoni-designed twin cylinder, double overhead cam Patons finally appeared in both 350 and 500cc form in 1967, ridden by Fred Stevens, who was sponsored by Liverpool car dealer Bill Hannah.

The 350 Aermacchi was beginning to give the 'British singles' a hard time in classic GPs. Aermacchi works riders, Alberto Pagani and Gilberto Milani, Australian Kel Carruthers, and the bored-out 250 MZs of Derek Woodman and Heinz Rosner were keeping privateers on Nortons and 7Rs out of the top six. The 250cc class was now two-stroke-dominated, with the water-cooled Bultaco earning its keep for many privateers such as Tommy Robb, Jack Findlay and Guyla Marsovsky, who were frequently in the top six in classic GPs. Ginger Molloy, now on a works Bultaco, and Tommy Robb were 4th and 5th in the Spanish GP, Jack Findlay and Guyla Marsovsky were 4th and 5th in the West German GP, Ginger Molloy was 6th in the Dutch TT, Molloy and Marsovsky were 5th and 6th in the Belgian and East German GPs, and Marsovsky was 4th in Finland. Likewise, the 125cc class was also made up of mainly two-strokes, apart from the private 125 CR93 Hondas of Kel Carruthers, Jim Curry, and German rider Walter Scheimann, who were often close rivals.

The usual suspects turned up on 23rd April at the Eifelrennen at the Nürburgring, where they were met with the usual snow and freezing conditions. Jack Findlay won the 500 race from Mike Duff on the Arter G50, and Mike won the 350

Johnny Dodds (Norton) in the Czech GP at Brno in 1968. (Courtesy Karl-Gunter Peters)

Dan Shorey (Norton) leading Mike Duff (Matchless) and Chris Conn (Norton) in the 1967 German GP at Hockenheim. (Courtesy Dan Shorey)

race after a last corner minor collision with John Blanchard's 7R. Jack Findlay also won the 250 race on his Bultaco, with Jim Curry getting a well-earned 2nd on his 182 Honda, and German rider Lothar John 3rd on a TR250 Suzuki. Jim Curry was also 4th in the 125 race, behind the three works Suzukis, with the other CR93 contender Giuseppe Visenzi 5th.

Earlier at Le Mans, on 19th April, Rob Fitton (Norton) won the 350 race and Billie Nelson also on a Norton won the 500, followed by Marsovsky's G50 and Chris Conn's Norton.

At the Dutch circuit of Tubbergen in May, Rudi Thalhammer (Aermacchi) won the 250 race, Marsovsky (Bultaco) was 2nd, and Jim Curry 3rd on his 182cc CR93. The 125 race was a three-cornered scrap between Cees van Dongen and Jim Curry on Hondas, and Sigfried Lohman on an MZ, with van Dongen getting the verdict from Jim Curry and Lohmann.

Jim Curry on his 182cc Honda at the start of the 1967 250 race at the Eifelrennen. (Courtesy Karl Schleuter)

At the 350 East German GP in 1967, Agostini walks to the start line, followed by L-R John Hartle (Aermacchi) Dan Shorey (Norton) and Fred Stevens (AJS). (Courtesy Dan Shorey)

Erstwhile sidecar passenger Billie Nelson (Norton) who was 3rd in the 1967 Finnish GP.

Jim Curry (182 Honda) in the 1967 Czech GP at Brno. (Courtesy Jarda Sejk)

Dan Shorey (Norton) leading Rex Butcher (Norton) and Gyula Marsovsky (Matchless) at the Sachsenring in 1968. (Courtesy Dan Shorey)

Meanwhile, in the World Championships, making another comeback after a series of injuries, John Hartle put up some remarkable performances towards the end of the season on Ray Cowles G50, when he finished 2nd in the East German, Finnish and Ulster GPs, plus other top six places, to take 3rd place in the 500cc World Championship. Peter Williams was in brilliant form, and was leading the 500cc World Championship on Tom Arter's G50 in the early stages, with 2nd place in the West German GP and the Senior TT, and 3rd in the Dutch TT, but fell off at the La Source hairpin in the

After the TT, Dutch TT and Belgian GP, the Circus regulars arrived at Jičín in Czechoslovakia in July, where Kel Carruthers, Jim Curry and Cees van Dongen on Hondas were involved in a three man scrap in the 125 race with Carruthers taking the win from Jim Curry after van Dongen fell off on the last corner.

Belgian GP. He then had a more serious crash at the Sachsenring in the East German GP, when he badly damaged an ankle. This put him out of action for the rest of the season, but he still finished 4th in the World Championships.

Yet another noteworthy performance in 1967 was put up by Jack Findlay, on the McIntyre

John Hartle (Ray Cowles Matchless) on which he was 3rd in the 500cc World Championships in 1967, with three brilliant 2nd places in East Germany, Finland and the Ulster GPs. (Courtesy Elwyn Roberts)

Circus regular Lewis Young who changed his Matchless to a G50 Metisse in 1968. (Courtesy Lewis Young)

MZ works rider Heinz Rosner at the Gooseneck in the 1968 Junior TT.

Matchless. He sustained injuries in a crash, during TT practice, when his Bultaco seized and threw him off on the approach to Quarter Bridge, which kept him out of the races. He paddle-started from the back of the grid at the Belgian GP, and clawed his way up to 4th place. In the East German GP he was involved in a battle for 2nd place with John Hartle, John Cooper and Australian Johnny Dodds, eventually finishing 3rd. In Czechoslovakia his Matchless gearbox seized during practice, and he fell heavily, sustaining head injuries. Undeterred, he was back again at the Ulster with a well earned 3rd place, eventually finishing 4th in the World Championships.

John Cooper and Billie Nelson kept the 500 Norton in the picture, with 3rd places in Czechoslovakia and Finland, respectively. Johnny Dodds, one of the new generation of Australian riders, put up some remarkable performances on the scruffiest looking Nortons, that included a hard fought 4th place in East Germany, and a 6th place in Czechoslovakia. Dan Shorey was 4th in the Dutch TT and 6th in the 350 East German on his Petty prepared Nortons and Gyula Marsovsky was another top six finisher on his G50 in the Belgian Dutch and Czech GPs. Fred Stevens on the Hannah Patons was 4th in the Dutch TT, and 6th in the Italian GP on the 350 version. On the 500cc version he was 3rd in the Belgian GP, 5th in Finland and 4th in the Italian GP. A sister machine, ridden by Angelo Bergamonti, was 3rd in the 500cc Italian GP.

Lewis Young (G50 Metisse) leading Fritzhof Eccarius (Norton), Dan Shorey (Norton) and Gyula Marsovsky (Matchless) at Hockenheim in 1968. (Courtesy Karl-Heinz Reiger)

Changes began to take place in 1968 that were a pointer to the future. One of the most significant developments in 1968 was undoubtedly Rod Gould's Ron Herring-built Bultaco/Yamaha special, a 250cc TD1C engine in a Bultaco frame, on which he eventually finished 4th in the 250 World Championships. This machine pre-dated the production TD2 and its larger brother the 350 TR2.

A typical Continental Circus start scene, with Ginger Molloy (250 Bultaco) getting away from #3 Renzo Passolini and #19 Gilberto Milani on Aermacchis.

The Aermacchi was now established as the best of the rest, with some riders opting for the alternative Rickman frame kits. Yet another Aermacchi frame kit was produced by the Swiss brothers Marly and Othmar Drixel, as used by Kel Carruthers on his Drixton. There were also signs that TD1C Yamahas and the Kawasaki were starting to gain in popularity.

Despite the threat from the two-strokes, most of the regular Circus privateers set out in their vans with their British single-cylinder machines, intent on earning their living as professional riders. Most of the usual suspects were still there; John Hartle, Jack Findlay, Dan Shorey, Ginger Molloy, Lewis Young, Robin Fitton, Billie Nelson, Gyula Marsovsky, Derek Woodman, Godfrey Nash, plus more recent additions including Rod Gould and New Zealander Keith Turner.

At Rimini on March 24th, John Hartle was 3rd in the 500 race on his G50 Metisse, behind Agostini's MV and Mike Hailwood's HRS Honda. At Le Mans on April 7th, Bill Smith won the 350 race on an ex-works Honda, and Kel Carruthers had two 2nd places on his 350 Aermacchi and 500 Norton. Rod Gould was 3rd on his 500 Norton, and Godfrey Nash 4th, also on a Norton. In the 500cc race Pierre Monneret, on a works MV, set a new lap record of 109.94mph (175.90km/h).

Over at Cesenatico in Italy, on the same day, at a wet meeting, John Cooper was 3rd in the 500cc on a Seely, followed by John Hartle (G50 Metisse), Billie Nelson (Paton) and Dan Shorey (Norton). A week later at Imola, John Cooper was 3rd again in the 500cc race at Imola behind Hailwood and Agostini. John Hartle was 5th, and Peter Williams 6th on the Arter Matchless.

German rider Lothar John on a Honda CR93.

John Cooper scored another 3rd at Cervia on April 25th, where Jack Findlay, Billie Nelson, and Peter Williams were 5th, 6th, and 7th.

After finishing 2nd in the 500cc West German GP on the Nürburgring South circuit, Dan Shorey headed to the Salzburg autobahn circuit on May 1st, where he was 3rd in the 350 race behind two works CZs, and 2nd in the 500 race, won by Billie Nelson on the Paton, with Johnny Dodds 3rd and Rod Gould 4th on Nortons. Rod Gould continued to gain success with the Bultaco/Yamaha, with 3rd place in the 250 race behind Ralph Bryans' Honda six and Laslo Szabo's MZ. The Toombs brothers, making one of their continental visits, were 6th in the sidecar race, with their BMW led by the inevitable BMW German crews.

John Cooper was having a good season on the Continent, with three wins at Tilburg on May 11/12, with a 250 Yamaha, and 350 and 500cc Seeleys to add to his 3rd places at Cesenatico and Imola. At Bourge-en-Bresse, on May 5th, Robin Fitton had a 500cc win, followed by Maurice Hawthorne (Norton) and Keith Turner (Matchless), Robin was also 3rd in the 350 race.

At Hockenheim on May 12th, Kel Carruthers and John Hartle were 3rd and 4th in the 350 race. Billie Nelson (Paton) was 2nd to Agostini in the 500cc race, followed by Rob Fitton, Dan Shorey, Jack Findlay on the McIntyre, and Johnny Dodds. In spite of the 'rough and ready' look of his Norton, it proved to be quite fast, and John Dodds had a 500cc win at Skofia Loka on May 25/26th. He followed this with another 500cc win at Tubbergen on June 3rd, where Robin Fitton had two 2nd places on his Nortons.

The Dutch meeting at Zolder in July was virtually dominated by the Circus riders, and was an indicator of the impending two-stroke invasion. Billie Nelson won the 250 race on his Doncaster Yamaha special, Jack Findlay was 2nd on a Bultaco, and Rex Butcher 3rd on a Suzuki. Jack Findlay won the 500 race on the McIntyre Matchless, Peter Williams was 2nd on the Arter Matchless, Billie Nelson was 3rd on the Paton, Derek Woodman 4th on a Seeley, Kel Carruthers

5th on his Norton and Ron Chandler 6th on a Seeley. To end the day Tony Wakefield and Graham Milton won the sidecar race with their BMW, followed by Kolle and Castella on BMWs.

Meanwhile Kiwi Ginger Molloy had been achieving remarkable results with the works Bultacos, that included a new air-cooled TSS350. On the 250 version he was 2nd in the West German, beating Kent Anderson and Rod Gould's Yamahas, 3rd in the Spanish, 5th in the East German, 4th in Finland and the Ulster, all of which earned him 4th place in the World Championship. He was also 5th in the 350 World Championships with 4th place in the West German, 2nd in the Dutch TT, and 4th in the East German. On the 125cc version he was 3rd in the World Championship, with two 2nd places in Spain and the Dutch TT, and 4th place in the Ulster.

The 125cc class was now virtually two-stroke-dominated, by the works and private MZs and Ginger Molloy's works Bultaco, followed by Kel Carruthers and Walter Scheimann on their CR93 Hondas, while the privateers in the 250cc class were mostly Bultaco mounted. The 350cc class saw an increase in the number of private Aermacchis. However, the classic British 'singles' were still the most successful privateer machine in the 500cc class. The Seeley derivations were also gaining in popularity with John Cooper, Derek Woodman, and Ron Chandler now on Seeley G50s. Jack Findlay was 2nd in the 500cc World Championship on the McIntyre Matchless, and popular Swiss-Hungarian Gyula Marsovsky was 3rd on his G50 Matchless.

One of the more consistent private riders was Leeds engineer Robin Fitton, who rode a very quick 500 Norton with which he had wins on the very fast Chimay circuit in 1965 and 1966. His engines were usually prepared pre-season by Bill Stuart, and later he used a Torsten Aagard five-speed gearbox. In spite of a couple serious accidents earlier in his career when he suffered a fractured skull at Regensdorf and a crash during TT practice in 1960, he achieved several wins and podium places on

Programme cover from the Belgian Grand Prix, July 7th, 1968.

Robin Fitton on his very fast 500 Norton. (Courtesy Elwyn Roberts)

the Continent. He was most successful in 1964, with wins at Tubbergen, Le Mans, Bourg-en-Bresse and Albi. In 1968, he was 4th in the 500cc World Championship with 4th place in the Belgian GP and 2nd place in the Ulster GP. Sadly, during practice for the 1970 German GP, he crashed and collided with the newly-installed Armco barrier, sustaining fatal injuries.

Chapter *19*

TWO-STROKE REVOLUTION

The impending two-stroke invasion gathered momentum in 1969, initially in the 250cc class. The introduction of the improved Yamaha TD1C in 1968, and the success of Rod Gould's Bultaco/Yamaha special, led to its increase in popularity among most private 250cc riders. Several TD1Cs were also increased in capacity for the 350cc class. Finally the TD2 Yamaha became available in 1969, to eventually become the definitive 250cc machine, followed by the 350cc TR2 Yamaha a year later. These two Japanese machines eventually changed the face of racing for the foreseeable future, and led to a rapid decline in the use of classic four-stroke machines among the private riders.

The 250cc GP class was now over-run with

Start of an Austrian GP on the Salzburg Autobahn circuit, with Gilberto Milani (Aermacchi) in the lead.

Yamahas, including the works TD2s of Rod Gould and Kent Anderson, with strong opposition from the lone Ossa of Spanish hero Santiago Herrero.

The single cylinder, six speed, air-cooled, disc valve Ossa had been developed by Eduardo Giro. The engine which was producing 40bhp at 11,000rpm, was mounted in a box section aluminium monocoque frame. However it was Australian Kel Carruthers who took over Renzo Passolini's four-cylinder Benelli and recorded the last ever 250cc World Championship GP win by a four stroke. In a dramatic final round at Opatija in Yugoslavia, when he snatched the title from Kent Andersson's works Yamaha, and a brave Herrero, who was riding with his left arm in plaster after a crash in the Ulster GP.

Dave Simmonds' 125cc World Championship, that included eight wins, was particularly remarkable, in spite of opposition from the ex-works Suzuki of Dieter Braun. Although ostensibly riding a works Kawasaki it was strictly a one-man effort, with Dave carrying out all his own maintenance throughout the season, and having only a limited supply of spares from Japan.

Meanwhile the privateers soldiered on with their four-stroke Nortons and Aermacchis. The early-season Italian meetings at Rimini, Modena and Riccioni, more or less set the scene of the two-stroke domination, apart from the Aermacchis of Gilberto Milani and Kel Carruthers.

At Le Mans in March 1969, it was Kel Carruthers again who won the 250/350 race on an Aermacchi. The new Lintos also made their first appearance at Le Mans. Keith Turner and Johnny Dodds had changed their Nortons for Lintos, and were 1st and 2nd respectively, while Gyula Marsovszky had

Walter Scheimann (Norton) at Nürburgring South in 1969. (Courtesy Karl-Gunter Peters)

Alan Barnett (Kirby Metisse), who was 3rd in the 1969 500cc Belgian GP. (Courtesy Elwyn Roberts)

also changed his Matchless for a Linto, on which he put up a new 500cc lap record of 112.94mph (181.72km/h). The ever-faithful Norton exponent Rob Fitton was 3rd, and Godfrey Nash was 5th on his Norton.

The new 500cc twin-cylinder Linto was basically the top half of two 250 Aermacchi engines mounted on a common crankcase and crankshaft assembly, and was designed by ex-Bianchi engineer Lino Tonti. The machines were initially much faster than the average 500 Norton or G50 Matchless, with an estimated maximum speed of 160mph (256km/h), that prompted several riders to opt for the Italian machine. Fast though the Linto undoubtedly was, it proved rather fragile, and it was the other Italian twin-cylinder machine, the Paton ridden by Billie Nelson, that proved more successful.

As far as the World Championships were concerned, it was Circus regular Godfrey Nash who finished 3rd in the 500cc events, after recording the last GP win for Norton in the Yugoslav GP, plus a 3rd in Finland, and two 5th places in Spain and France. Alan Barnett was 4th in the World Championships on a Kirby G50 Metisse, following his 2nd place in the Senior TT, and 3rd place in the Dutch TT. The Belgian GP at Spa Francorchamps featured a fierce, race-long battle for 2nd place between Alan Barnett's Seeley and Percy Tait on the new works Triumph Dayton. Barnett's Seeley went off song towards the end of the race, and he had to settle for 3rd place behind Percy Tait's Triumph. Peter Williams, having a one-off GP ride, was 2nd in the Dutch TT on the Arter Matchless behind Agostini's MV.

At the Imola International on April 7th,

Kel Carruthers was 2nd to Agostini's MV on a 382cc Aermacchi, while John Cooper, who had stuck to his Seeley, was 3rd. The ever-cheerful Jim Curry, who was now riding a 350 Aermacchi Metisse, recorded his first GP win at the Nürburgring Nordschleifer on April 26th. At Bourg-en-Bresse on 27th April, John Cooper won the 500 race on his Seeley and was 2nd in the 350 race. In the Austrian GP on the usual Autobahn circuit on May 4th, perennial Circus rider Lewis Young was 2nd in the 350 race on an Aermacchi Metisse. The 500 race was won by Karl Hoppe, with the Helmut Fath engine URS/Metisse, while John Dodds was 2nd on his Linto, and Billie Nelson was 3rd on a Paton.

At Keimola, Finland, in August, Lewis Young fought a losing battle against the Yamahas and Herrero's Ossa, to finish 3rd in the 350 race, followed by Billie Nelson, and a young Barry Sheene on a Bultaco. In the 500 race, John Dodds was 2nd on his Linto, with Godfrey Nash (Norton) 3rd, and Terry Dennehey 4th on one of the new Drixton/Hondas: a Honda 450 engine in a Drixton frame, built by New Zealander Ray Breingan.

The Czech GP on August 24th was run at Jičín, where Ginger Molloy won the 125 race on a Bultaco.

Jack Findlay had sold the McIntyre Matchless to Austrian Willi Berghold, and invested in a 350 Yamaha. Another who opted for Yamaha power was German Circus regular Walter Scheimann, formerly a staunch Norton man. The 350 Aermacchi was now hard pushed to get into the top six in the Classic GPs, but still achieved some success, mainly due to the efforts of Kel Carruthers on the works machines, including a 382cc version.

Gyula Marsovszky finished 2nd in the 500cc World Championships on his Linto, with some steady top six places, and a 2nd in the Czech GP at Brno, in spite of a crash in the Freiburg Hillclimb in July that put him out of action until September, with concussion, broken ribs and a broken collar bone. Jack Findlay was due to ride the works Linto, but due to its unreliability he was forced to resort to various other machines. It was not Jack's year. He crashed Tom Arter's G50 in the Belgian GP, and crashed again later in the year while riding the ex- Bill Ivy works V4 Jawa. Ironically, in spite of what was a somewhat unlucky season, Jack was the main subject of the excellent film *Continental Circus* by French film-maker Jérôme Laperrousaz.

Since 1963, Lewis Young had been a regular Continental Circus privateer, riding his Tom Kirby sponsored 7R and G50. As a full-time professional racer, he was one of the most knowledgeable on all aspects of racing on the Continent. Over the years he had his fair share of success, including several top six places in the classic GPs, particularly in Eastern Europe and Scandinavia, where he chose to do much of his racing. His agreement with Tom Kirby ended in 1968, and in 1969 he rode a 350 Drixton Aermacchi and a Drixton/Honda, on which he was 5th in the Finnish GP and 4th in the Yugoslavian GP, before retiring at the end of the year.

Among the sidecar brigade, Continental involvement was quite sparse, but Tony Wakefield and Graham Milton (BMW) were 3rd in the Eifelrennen at the Nürburgring in April, and 6th in the West German GP at Hockenheim. Graham Milton, now with a sister BMW outfit and John Thornton as passenger, was 6th in the Belgian GP, followed by Tony Wakefield and John Flaxman in 7th place with the other BMW. Dick Hawes and John Mann were 10th in the West German, and 7th in the French GP, with their Seeley/G50 outfit. Pat Coxon (BMW) won the sidecar race at Bourg-en-Bresse on May 4th.

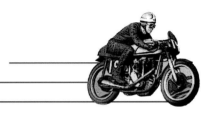

During 1970, with the exception of Agostini's 350 MV and Renzo Passolini's Benelli, the 250 and 350cc classes were dominated by the Yamahas of Rod Gould, Kel Carruthers, Kent Anderson and Jarno Saarinen, followed by dozens of other Yamahas, now ridden by Tommy Robb, Jack Findlay, Billie Nelson, Ginger Molloy, Gyula Marsovszky, and others too numerous to mention. The 350cc four-stroke works Aermacchis had disappeared from the scene, soon to be replaced by the new two-stroke versions. However, Alan Barnett and Jim Curry stuck to their Aermacchis. Apart from his 2nd place in the Junior TT, Alan Barnett did well to finish amongst the first ten Yamahas in East Germany and Ulster. Jim Curry was 6th in the West German GP and 10th in the Dutch TT on his Aermacchi. The 500cc class was a mixture of machines including Linto, Paton, G50 Seeley, G50 Matchless and Norton.

Foremost among the Seeley riders was Tommy Robb, demonstrating that he was not only a 125 and 250cc rider, by finishing 4th in the 500cc World Championships with podium places in West Germany and Belgium, and several other top six places. Another successful Seeley rider was Alan Barnett who was 2nd in the West German GP, and 4th in the East German. The 500cc class was now under attack from the two-strokes. Ginger Molloy started the season with an oversize Bultaco, before switching to a Kawasaki on which he came 2nd in the French, Finnish and Spanish GPs, to finish 2nd in the World Championship.

At the Italian GP in September, the MVs of Agostini and Bergamonti were followed by eight Kawasakis. Godfrey Nash persevered with his Norton, and Billie Nelson stayed with the Hannah Paton. Gyula Marsovszky was not as successful with the Linto as the previous year, although Johnny Dodds was 2nd in East Germany on his Linto. Lewis Young was 5th in the Belgian GP on his Drixton Honda, and Terry Dennehy was 6th on a sister machine.

By the early 1970s, many of the minor Circus events were no longer run. Well-known traditional circuits such as St Wendel, Solitude, Salzburg Autobahn, Cadours, Albi, Clermont Ferrand, Imatra, and Helsinki, to name a few, eventually disappeared. Switzerland lost all its circuits when racing was banned after the Le Mans disaster. A fatal accident involving Angelo Bergamonti at Riccione in April 1971, led to Italy banning racing on street circuits. Consequently, the circuits used for the traditional early season Adriatic meetings at Riccione, Cesenatico, Rimini, Senigallia, and others, were abandoned.

Although some private riders continued to ride in Grand Prix events into the 1970s, many different factors now began to affect the future for private riders wishing to earn a living by racing in the non-championship events – chiefly the loss of the circuits, at which the privateers earned most of their start money.

The removal of advertising constraints had opened the door to lucrative sponsorship deals for the factory teams. The excesses soon began, with large sums of money being spent on publicity, corporate identity, hospitality, race transporters, motor homes etc. While all this undoubtedly raised the standard of Grand Prix Racing for the privileged factory riders, the sheer cost made it unsustainable for the ordinary privateers. A combination of all these factors led to the eventual demise of the real Continental Circus, which had essentially consisted of private riders who raced to earn a living in non-GP events all over Europe.

Mike Hailwood making a typical start in the German GP at Hockenheim, followed by the rest of the Circus, including #4 Agostini, #6 Peter Williams, #4 Robin Fitton, #37 Mike Duff, and #21 Fred Stevens.

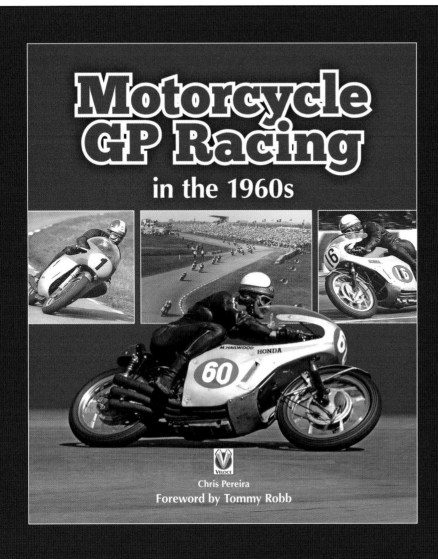

More great motorcycling stories from Veloce:

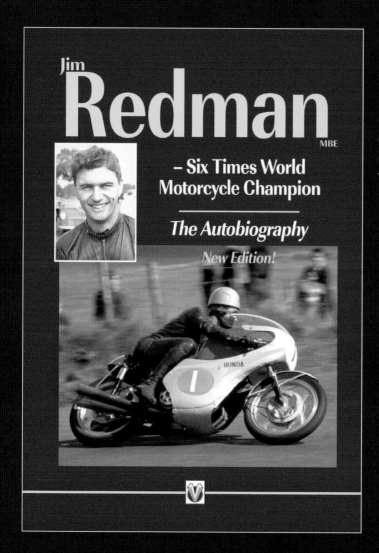

"*Any fan of motorcycle racing will find* Jim Redman: Six Times World Champion *absorbing; any fan of true stories of grit and determination overcoming impossible odds will find it hard to put down.*"
– UltimateMotorcycling.com

The incredible rags-to-riches story of one of the world's greatest motorcycle racers. From humble beginnings to winning six world titles, Jim Redman MBE is one of GP's most extraordinary characters, and a true legend of motorcycle racing. This book is a fascinating and compelling autobiography. (Paperback edition)

ISBN: 978-1-787110-44-1
Paperback • 22.5x15.2cm • 304 pages • fully illustrated

For more information and price details, visit our website at www.veloce.co.uk

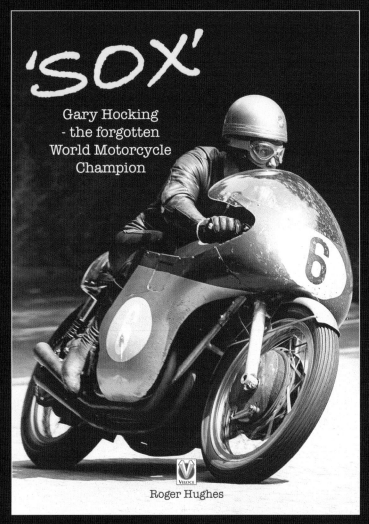

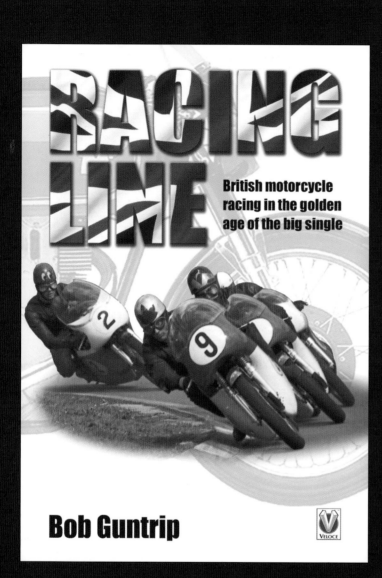

Index

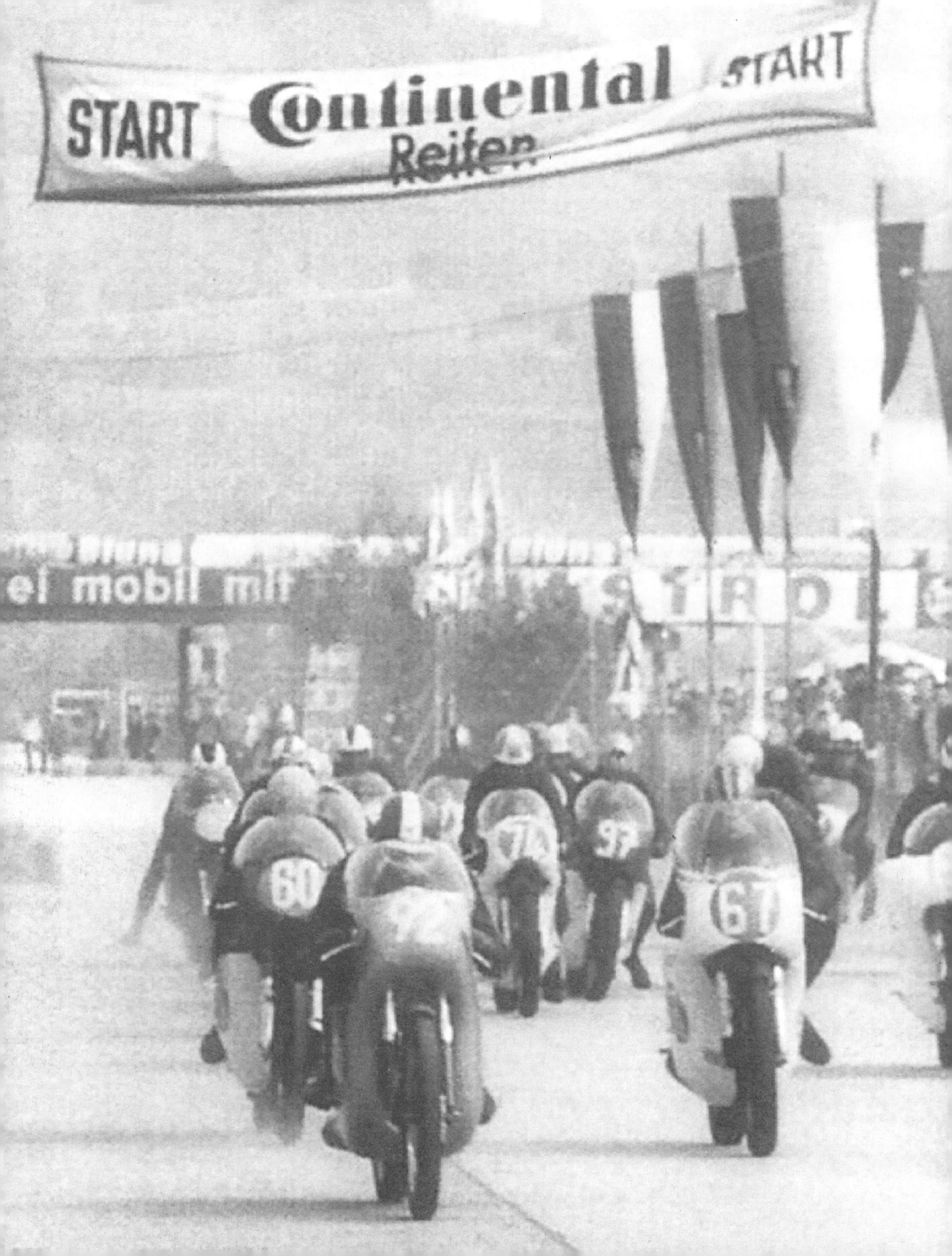
START
Continental
Reifen
START
el mobil mit
60
74
97
67